The Home Town Advantage

The Home Town Advantage

How to Defend Your Main Street Against Chain Stores ... And Why It Matters

STACY MITCHELL

Institute for Local Self-Reliance

MINNEAPOLIS, MN   WASHINGTON, D.C.

The New Rules Project identifies and promotes policies that nurture healthy communities and strong local economies. The project is a comprehensive effort to articulate a new vision of politics and economics for the twenty-first century. The New Rules Project is a program of the Institute for Local Self-Reliance, a 25-year-old nonprofit research and educational organization that provides technical assistance and information on environmentally sound economic development strategies.

For more information about the New Rules Project, including a list of other titles, please visit our Web site at **www.newrules.org** or contact us at:

Institute for Local Self-Reliance

1313 5th Street SE
Minneapolis, MN 55414
Phone: 612-379-3815
Fax: 612-379-3920
www.ilsr.org

2425 18th Street NW
Washington, DC 20009
Phone: 202-232-4108
Fax: 202-332-0463

Illustrations by Ken Avidor.
Book design by Barb Koster and David Steinlicht.

ISBN 0-917582-89-6

1 2 3 4 5 6 7 8 9 0

Table of Contents

Acknowledgments

Most importantly, I want acknowledge the contribution of Institute for Local Self-Reliance co-founder David Morris, who deserves credit for much of the inspiration and many of the ideas behind this book. I would also like to thank him for providing crucial feedback along the way.

I would like to thank the many people who provided information, assistance, and insight for this book, especially those who reviewed it in draft form: Marcia Keller Avner, Linda Davidoff, Richard Kazis, Lee A. Krohn, and Jeff Milchen. Any errors that remain, of course, are the sole responsibility of the author.

I also want to thank my colleagues at ILSR, especially Daniel Kraker, Pam Neary, and Corinne Rafferty for their contributions, and Elizabeth Noll, whose editing and production oversight improved the final product considerably.

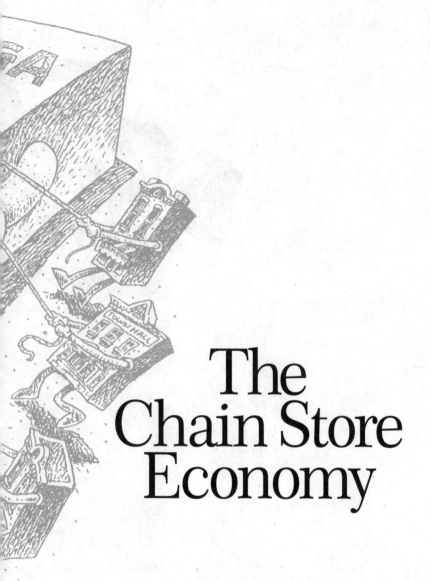

The
Chain Store
Economy

Trends are Not Destiny

When people lament the disappearance of the local bookseller or neighborhood pharmacist, too often they speak with a deep sense of resignation. We mourn the loss, but deep in our hearts we accept these enterprises' extinction as an inevitable part of market evolution. We take as self-evident that giant chains, with their MBAs and sophisticated computer systems and vast buying power and global reach, can and do offer us more convenience, a wider selection, better service, and lower prices. We take as self-evident that chains create jobs in sleepy, stagnant rural economies and generate additional tax revenues for public services.

But when subjected to empirical scrutiny, these received truths turn out to be far less compelling. Large chains reduce the existing diversity of locally owned shops, leaving the economy and the customer at the mercy of an absentee-owned firm that can raise prices or abandon the

1

community in later years. Local officials who eagerly court giant retailers with handsome tax incentives and grants may discover that the public costs outweigh the public gains.

We live in a dynamic, churning economy. A market economy guarantees no business perpetual life. Retail and service businesses aggressively compete to capture a share of the $2.3 trillion consumers spend annually. But in the last two decades retail ownership has undergone a dramatic shift: from local, independent merchants to national chains. Books, groceries, office supplies, hardware, pharmaceuticals and many other goods are now sold primarily through giant retail companies.

Sometimes this is a result of market forces—the efficient displacing the inefficient. But just as often it is a result of large corporations being given advantages that tilt the playing field. When Barnes & Noble receives price breaks from publishers far below those justified by the reduced costs of their larger book orders, it is gaining an advantage over local bookstores that is not only unfair but illegal under current antitrust statutes. When Wal-Mart sets up shop on the outskirts of town and receives millions of dollars in free roads and land and sewers and tax abatements it is gaining an unfair and unwarranted advantage over local businesses who are, in effect, seeing their taxes going to subsidize a competitor. When Amazon.com can sell books over the internet and avoid paying state and local sales taxes, it is gaining a 6-8 percent price advantage over local businesses.

Public policy often discriminates against locally owned enterprises. We argue that it should discriminate in their favor.

Local businesses enrich the civic fabric. Small merchants care about their communities more because they are part of those communities. The taxes they pay provide services, like schools and police and parks, that they and their families use. Small merchants give to community causes more than their big competitors. Their purchases and profits tend to circulate within and strengthen the local economy rather than flowing to distant suppliers or corporate headquarters.

The trends, as we shall see in the opening chapter of this report, are dismal. But trends are not destiny. Concentration occurs only when we allow it to occur and currently public policy not only allows absentee ownership, it actively encourages it.

It is time to change the rules. Local merchants still command a significant share of the market for consumer goods and services, but, with economic consolidation proceeding at a staggering pace, citizens need to act now to ensure the survival of local retail and service businesses. A number of communities have taken the lead in fashioning policies that favor diverse, humanly scaled, locally owned, autonomous businesses. This book describes the tools they are using and discusses ways in which local businesses, in partnership with local governments, can once again become a key component in a healthy, dynamic, and rooted retail sector.

Examples of the policies described in this publication—including the full text of laws and relevant court cases, background material, resources, links, and news—can be found on the New Rules web site at **www.newrules.org**.

CHAPTER one

The Retail Sector Consolidates

The market share of corporate chains has been expanding at a staggering pace. More than 5 percent of *all* retail spending is now captured by a single chain, Wal-Mart. The third largest corporation in the U.S., Wal-Mart generated $138 billion in sales in 1998, more than three times the revenue of the next largest retailer. Wal-Mart also ranks as the fourth largest grocer in the country. The chain has grown from 275 outlets in 1980 to 3,500 today.[1]

Wal-Mart, along with rivals Kmart and Dayton Hudson's Target, are known as discount mass merchandisers, a fiercely competitive breed of retailers that stock an extensive variety of general merchandise and recently have grown to include grocery departments, pharmacies, and fast-food outlets. These massive stores typically range from 90,000 to 250,000 square feet, two to five times the size of a football field and 20 to 50 times the size of typical downtown retailer.[2]

Beyond the mass merchandisers are the category killers, stores that sell an in-depth selection of one type of merchandise. These companies are relative newcomers to the retail scene; many did not expand significantly until the 1990s. Yet the category killers, as their name suggests, have gobbled up substantial market shares in their respective categories while their independent competitors are on the decline.

More than 25 percent of all U.S. book sales are captured by two firms, Barnes & Noble and Borders Books. In 1972, independent booksellers claimed 58 percent of all book sales, but by 1997, their share had fallen to just 17 percent.[3] While many communities have lost their neighborhood hardware stores, Home Depot sustained revenue gains of 36 percent annually between 1985 and 1995. Home Depot and its competitor, Lowe's, generated combined sales of $42 billion in 1998 at just over 1,200 outlets. These two giants now account for nearly one-quarter of hardware and building supply sales.[4] Category killers have emerged in nearly every product group. Electronics are dominated by Circuit City and Best Buy. Office Max, Office Depot, and Staples have taken over much of the office supply business, while the market share of small and medium-sized office products stores has fallen from 20 percent to just 4 percent since 1986.[5]

Like the mass merchandisers, category killers tend operate on a large scale. Home Depot stores generally exceed 100,000 square feet. Borders Books and Barnes & Noble stores range from 20,000 to 45,000 square feet, compared to the 1,500 to 7,000 square foot size of a typical independent bookstore.

Although large stores like Wal-Mart and Home Depot may be the most visible examples of corporate retail growth, the chaining of America is proceeding rapidly in smaller-scale retail functions as well. Walgreen, CVS, and

Rite Aid have a combined total of 10,000 stores and $43 billion in annual revenue. Meanwhile, community pharmacies have been failing at a rate of about 1,000 per year for the last five years. Today, independents account for less than 17 percent of retail pharmacy sales while chain stores and mail order firms absorb an ever-larger share of the market.[6] Starbucks operates nearly 2,000 coffee shops in North America and Blockbuster Video accounts for 30 percent of U.S. video rental sales.[7] Two hundred restaurant chains capture more than 40 percent of the $308 billion U.S. food service market.[8]

Other corporations, known as "consolidators" or "rollup" firms, have taken a more stealth approach to expansion by buying up existing retail stores. U.S. Office Products, for instance, owns several hundred formerly independent office supply stores. These small and medium-sized businesses usually continue to give the appearance of local ownership, often retaining their original name. In actuality they are locally managed, but absentee-owned.[9]

Another substantial portion of the retail and service sector is occupied by franchise businesses, which are especially prevalent in the fast-food industry, but also include many other businesses like gas stations and hotels. About one out of five outlets in a typical franchise chain is owned by the company. Although the remainder are ostensibly locally owned, these small businesspeople have lost much their autonomy in the last fifteen years as franchise corporations exert ever greater control over the business and often reap the bulk of the financial rewards.

The size and market power of the nation's top retail and service corporations have made them formidable competitors to independent merchants. By purchasing goods in large quantities, often directly from manufacturers, national chains can substantially reduce their merchandise costs. Integrated warehousing and distribution systems, sophisticated information technologies, and centralized management, accounting, and legal functions further amplify the cost advantages corporate chains have over their smaller rivals.

Information technologies allow national retailers to instantaneously track inventory and sales in each of their stores. Often these systems are linked directly to major suppliers, allowing for precise timing of deliveries and minimizing the costs of warehouse storage and inventory maintenance. Indeed these systems can reduce the cost of moving goods from manufacturers to the retail floor by as much as 20 to 30 percent.[10] Information technologies also ensure that each store is stocked with the right quantity and mix of inventory, thereby avoiding lost sales due to insufficient supplies as well as markdowns necessary to reduce excess inventory.

National retailers have altered the dynamics of the distribution system. By operating their own distribution and warehousing facilities, and buying directly from manufacturers, large retailers circumvent wholesalers, distributors, and brokers, eliminating a portion of the logistical costs built into a traditional small retailer's operations. Wholesalers and distributors are rendered less efficient and less profitable by the decrease in the volume of goods they handle, which in turn may indirectly raise the costs for small retailers who depend on them.[11]

Worse still, many distributors are closing their doors. The number of grocery wholesalers has declined from 400 in 1981 to just 97 today.[12] As one small merchant said, "The large retailers buy directly from the manufacturer and eliminate the distributors. We can not compete under those circumstances. If we do not have distributors to supply us with merchandise, and we can not buy from the manufacturers, that doesn't hold much of a future for small businesses."[13] Some independent retailers have been reduced to purchasing their goods from "warehouse" retail stores, such as Costco or Wal-Mart-owned Sam's Club.

In the book industry, Barnes & Noble recently attempted to purchase Ingram Book Group, the nation's largest book distributor. Ingram is the primary supplier for independent bookstores and helps them track inventory and sales. Although the deal was ultimately dropped, it is another example of how retail consolidation threatens to compromise the distribution system that enables local merchants to operate.[14]

The growth in size and market share of national retailers has given them unprecedented power in their dealings with manufacturers. Barnes & Noble and Borders Books, for instance, generate more revenue than the top ten publishers combined. Rubbermaid, Inc., a $2 billion company, derives 15 percent of its sales from Wal-Mart. It is not alone. Other manufacturers who depend on the retailer for a substantial portion of their income include Fruit of the Loom (16 percent), Toastmaster (28 percent), and Armor All Products (20 percent).[15]

For fear of having their products pulled from the shelves, manufacturers tread carefully when dealing with the megastores, which don't hesitate to use their clout to demand deeper discounts, special deals for new store openings, and even payment of fines for shipping errors.[16] Many manufacturers, for instance, offer a 2 percent discount for invoices paid within 15 days. Wal-Mart routinely pays its invoices in 30 days, but takes the discount anyway. According to one manufacturing executive, "In terms of pricing, merchandising and slotting fees, the big discounters have pretty big sticks right now."[17]

As with wholesalers, small manufacturers are increasingly left out of the loop. A number of large retail companies, including Wal-Mart in 1991, have terminated their relationships with independent sales representatives, who typically market products for several small or mid-size manufacturers and are often the only affordable means for these companies to employ an outside sales force.[18]

Another concern looming on the horizon for local merchants is the growth of internet commerce. On-line retail sales climbed from $1 billion in 1997 to nearly $8 billion in 1998. Internet sales are currently exempt from sales taxes, meaning that those who shop at local stores will pay a 6 to 8 percent premium.[19]

CHAPTER two

The Benefits of Local Ownership

Many believe that the expansion of chain stores has been beneficial. Indeed corporate retailers have brought innovation to some sectors. Bigness does command certain efficiencies and increased competition has forced less competitive retail and service providers to streamline operations, improve service, stay open longer, trim prices, and expand product lines. But before the last independent store closes its doors, it's worth evaluating the claims of corporate retailers—namely that they bring consumers lower prices, wider selection, and greater convenience—and examining how the shift from local to absentee-owned businesses impacts communities and local economies.

As discussed in the previous chapter, national retailers

can be highly efficient, but how much of these reduced costs are passed on to consumers and for how long? National chains tend to price low when entering a new market and, unlike their independent competitors, can afford to operate at a loss for many months. In some cases, chains will price entire lines below acquisition costs, as Wal-Mart has done with its pharmacy department, in order to gain market share. Once rivals have been eliminated, prices tend to rise.[1]

In Virginia, a survey of pricing on specific items in a number of Wal-Mart stores about 30 to 40 miles apart found variations of as much as 25 percent. The researchers concluded that prices were lower in or near large competitive markets and tended to rise in smaller markets with limited competition.[2] Similar conclusions have been reached in surveys of Home Depot. One analyst compared prices on 35 items at a Home Depot in Atlanta with a store in Greensboro, North Carolina. Prices in Atlanta, where the retailer faces little competition, were 9.7 percent higher than in the more competitive Greensboro market.[3]

Large retailers often sell certain items below-cost as "loss leaders" to draw consumers into the store. This practice may apply to an entire category of goods. "Supercenters," which combine grocery store merchandise with general merchandise, often sell food products below-cost or at very slim margins with the idea that the increased traffic will cross over into the higher margin general merchandise.[4] Although consumers benefit from the lower grocery prices, this practice makes it very difficult for nearby grocery stores to compete, and ultimately consumers will be left with fewer choices.

In a lawsuit brought by three independent pharmacists against Wal-Mart in Conway, Arkansas, the court found that Wal-Mart had consistently priced up to 30 percent of its pharmaceutical and health and beauty aids below its own acquisition costs, making it impossible for local pharmacies to match the superstore's prices. With deep pockets and pharmacy goods accounting for only a portion of its inventory, Wal-Mart was able to sustain this practice for several years. Again, consumers were blessed with lower prices, but likely at the expense of a competitive market over the long-term. The court also concluded that Wal-Mart was selling goods at very low prices in competitive markets such as Conway or Little Rock, but in rural towns like Clinton and Flippen, where competition was minimal, the same items were sold at much higher prices.[5]

A large-scale retailer will initially provide a community with a big boost in terms of selection and convenience—sometimes doubling a small town's total retail space. Developers often present these stores as major additions to the local economy, but in areas with anything less than spectacular population and income growth, the bulk of the new store's sales will be taken directly from existing merchants and ultimately entail numerous small business failures. One study, for instance, examined nine Iowa counties where Wal-Mart had located and found that 84 percent of the megastore's sales were captured from existing businesses within the same county.[6]

Small, locally owned businesses provide economic diversity and stability. A town of 10,000 might support 50 to 60 small merchants, but when a large corporate retailer moves in, the host community as well as several smaller towns in the vicinity often lose their Main Street merchants altogether, leaving many of the region's residents little option but to travel long distances for even the most basic of daily necessities.[7]

This dependency carries risks. While local merchants will do their best to weather economic hard times, absentee owners are far more mobile and will abandon a community if profit margins do not meet their expectations. Such is the case in Warr Acres, a community of 10,000 located about 25 miles from downtown Oklahoma City. In 1992, local officials used public funds to convince Wal-Mart to open a 120,000 square foot store in their town. The opening led to several failures at existing businesses, including the loss of the local grocery store. Just six years later, Wal-Mart decided to close its doors in favor of opening a 200,000 square foot supercenter closer to Oklahoma City. Warr Acres will lose 8 percent of the its tax base.[8]

Communities left with an empty "big box" often have a hard time finding a new use for the property. Increasingly, national retailers are closing existing outlets in order to open larger stores in the same markets. Wal-Mart has more than 300 vacant stores in the U.S. Kansas City counts 26 vacant superstores within its borders, totaling 1.5 million square feet.[9]

Because of their size and impact on public revenue streams, corporate retailers often make demands that local governments find hard to refuse, a practice that subverts local democratic processes in favor of private interests. One of countless examples occurred in early 1998 when Costco, a $22 billion corporation, wanted to expand its store in Martinez, California. The retailer insisted that the city provide $2 million in tax rebates over several years to finance the construction or Costco would close the Martinez location. Sales taxes from the store amount to more than 5 percent of the city's budget. Most local governments in this position hand over the cash. Thanks to media attention and a subsequent public outcry, Martinez officials took the unusual step of denying Costco's request. The retailer has followed through on its threat, however, and plans to move a few miles away to the neighboring town of Concord.[10]

Providing tax breaks or subsidies for corporate retailers has become fairly commonplace.[11] The state of New York recently announced that Wal-Mart will be opening a distribution center in Johnstown. State taxpayers will be providing nearly $1 million in grants and another $1 million in road improvements on top of county-funded water and other public service expansions.[12] In Long Beach, California, city officials agreed to forgive $6 million in sales taxes over a period of fifteen years to attract a shopping center development that includes Kmart.[13]

Corporate retailers often play neighboring communities off one another to exact the biggest subsidies, a tactic perfected by Wal-Mart in the early days of its expansion and now utilized by many companies that find sales and property tax dependent local governments easy targets. Government support for these retailers delivers a double

14

blow to local businesses. Rarely are public funds made available to local merchants. Subsides instead help fuel the expansion of their biggest competitors.

Corporate retailers and public officials insist that these expenditures are justified as a means of generating new jobs and higher tax revenue. Unlike new manufacturing facilities, however, these gains will invariably be offset by job and tax losses at existing retailers, producing only marginal overall improvement or even a net decline in some cases. Even without additional subsidies, the public cost of development—expanding roads and providing services such as water and sewer—combined with declines in property values and sales taxes in existing retail centers may actually exceed the tax revenue generated by the new retailer.

One study paid for by Wal-Mart concluded that the superstore's proposal to locate in Greenfield, Massachusetts would cost existing businesses $35 million in sales, leading to a *net* loss of 105,000 square feet of retail space and consequently declines in property tax revenue. The 177 new jobs expected to be gained by the addition of Wal-Mart would be off-set by losses of 148 jobs at other businesses.[14]

Another study, which examined the impact of a proposed Wal-Mart in North Elba, New York, found that $12.3 million, or 68 percent, of the store's projected sales would be captured from local businesses. The 134 jobs promised by Wal-Mart would cause 112 job losses elsewhere, leaving the town with a net gain of only 22 jobs.[15]

A detailed study on the effects of a proposed Wal-Mart store in St. Albans, Vermont, concluded that the development would lead to a substantial decline in local government revenue. The study found that 76 percent of the new store's sales would be drawn from existing businesses in the county, leading to a net loss of 110,000 square feet of retail space and 167 jobs over a period of ten years. The failure of these businesses would result in a net decline in real and personal property values of $1.4 million countywide and significant reductions in property and payroll taxes.[16] In rejecting Wal-Mart's plans, the Vermont Environmental Board concluded that for each dollar of public benefits generated by the proposed store there would be 2.5 dollars in public costs.[17]

Despite evidence that megastores harm local businesses, one of the chief arguments that corporate retailers use when presenting development proposals to local planning agencies is that a large store will draw consumers from a wide radius, benefiting existing businesses with increased traffic and boosting the town's overall retail sales. This may have been true at one time when a new superstore could still command novelty appeal in many regions, drawing consumers from as far as 50 or 60 miles. But these retailers are opening hundreds of outlets every year, rapidly filling in the gaps between stores and saturating regional markets. The impact of large-scale stores may still spill out beyond a town's borders, but, as markets become saturated, trade areas shrink and much of a new store's sales will be derived from a much more localized market.[18]

Furthermore, chain stores, particularly large discount retailers and category killers, prefer to build on the outskirts of town or in suburban locations, rather then locating downtown or in neighborhood business districts. By drawing traffic away from existing retail centers, chain stores not only harm those local businesses that carry similar goods, but can negatively impact the sales of other stores that are not in direct competition. Ultimately, the effect on central business districts may be substantial and chronic vacancies, which not only represent an inefficient allocation of public and private resources, but further magnify the difficulties of surviving businesses by reducing the area's appeal to consumers. When downtown areas lose their economic viability, important cultural and historic structures may be left vacant with their survival threatened.

The North Elba Planning Board, after reviewing the results of the study cited above, rejected Wal-Mart's proposal, concluding, "The project will likely result in a large amount of impacted retail space, which could take up to 14 years to refill, over 20,000 s.f. of which could become chronically vacant. These potential impacts would have a significant unmitigatable adverse impact on the character and culture of the community by resulting in vacant storefronts, a loss of 'critical mass' in existing downtown areas, and an adverse psychological, visual and economic climate."[19]

Vacancies, job losses, and declines in public revenue are only part of the drain on local economies caused by the failure of independent businesses. Local ownership means that profits circulate within the community, and, unlike national chain stores, independent merchants patronize small regional distributors and wholesalers, and rely on other local businesses for services such as banking, printing, and accounting. National retailers bypass local providers and centralize these functions at their head offices.

Locally owned retail and service businesses provide qualitative benefits to communities unmatched by their corporate counterparts. Sustaining a small-scale, independent retail economy maintains broad ownership of local resources and ensures that business decisions are made locally by community members rather than occurring in distant board rooms. Local merchants have a vested interest in the health of the places in which they do business. They are linked to the community and invested in its governance in a variety of ways; the property taxes their businesses pay support the government services, like public schools, that their families use. Many small business owners contribute to the civic life of the community, sponsoring Little League teams and participating in community organizations. Small firms donate more financial support and volunteer time to charitable causes than large corporations.[20]

Communities are increasingly finding that saving a few bucks often comes at a very high price. Many have begun to look for ways to use public policy to sustain and nurture a more rooted, homegrown economy. This by no means entails preserving existing businesses at the expense of innovation and progress. In fact, the argument for a homegrown economy composed of diverse and numerous small businesses is an argument for a healthy, competitive market.

Changing the Rules

CHAPTER three

Reviving Antitrust

While legitimate economies of scale have allowed corporate retailers to aggressively compete, concerns are mounting that some have crossed the line, violating antitrust laws by using their market power to eliminate rivals. Anticompetitive practices were very much on the minds of the delegates at the 1995 White House Conference on Small Business, who felt that the government was not doing enough to investigate potential violations and enforce antitrust laws. The delegates passed the following resolution:

> Small business cannot compete with large businesses who use their economic power to extract unfair competitive pricing from manufacturers and service providers. Antitrust laws should be strength-

ened and enforced to prohibit abuses including unfair vertical integration, tying of pricing and product purchases, and predatory pricing tactics.

Independent retailers who have been victimized by anticompetitive practices, however, will have a difficult if not impossible time seeking relief. Although antitrust laws were originally enacted for the purpose of maintaining a decentralized economy of many small, independent businesses, today federal enforcement and judicial interpretation gives little consideration to this goal, focusing instead on maximizing efficiency and lowering consumer prices. Federal authorities have grown reluctant to aggressively enforce antitrust laws, believing that the efficiencies that accompany large corporations far outweigh any other social or economic consequences of market concentration. The courts have repeatedly raised the standard required to prove antitrust violations.

The Shifting Objectives of Antitrust Law

Unlike the narrow focus on consumer welfare that dominates today's thinking about antitrust policy, these laws were initially enacted with both an economic and civic purpose in mind.[1] Maintaining a decentralized economy of numerous small businesses ensured healthy competition and innovation by dispersing wealth, limiting business size, and broadening economic opportunities. It was also considered compatible with self-government—as opposed to concentrated economic power, which was considered a threat to democracy. As Senator John Sherman put it in 1890, "If we will not endure a king as a political power we should not endure a king over the production, transportation, and sale of the necessaries of life."[2]

Certainly antitrust policy was concerned with protecting consumers from monopoly pricing, but even if concentrated economic power proved a more efficient way to do business, the threat it posed to self-government and the possibility of that power being used to subvert government to the will of private interests rather than the public good was too great a risk. In a 1952 Senate debate on fair trade laws, Senator Hubert Humphrey denied that such laws led to higher prices, but went on to say:

> We are not necessarily talking about whether some penny-pinching person is going to be able to save half a cent on a loaf of bread. We are talking about the kind of America we want. Do we want an America where, on the highways and byways, all we have is catalog houses? Do we want an America where the economic market place is filled with a few Franken-steins and giants? Or do we want an America where there are thousands upon thousands of small entre-preneurs, independent businessmen, and landhold-ers who can stand on their own feet and talk back to their Government or to anyone else.[3]

The civic orientation of antitrust law began to fade after the 1950s. Today, antitrust policy is little concerned with maintaining a decentralized economy, but instead has focused almost exclusively on maximizing efficiency and protecting consumer welfare.[4] Courts view prices as the primary, if not exclusive, measure for assessing consumer welfare. If a large retailer sells goods below its acquisition costs or pressures suppliers for special discounts, then consumers benefit from lower prices. Although antitrust law prohibits predatory pricing and discriminatory dis-counts when used to injure competition, the judicial sys-tem is extremely reluctant to declare practices which pro-duce lower prices anticompetitive. As a result, the courts have set an almost impossibly high standard for proving such tactics illegal. The Justice Department and Federal Trade Commission (FTC) have likewise been reluctant to aggressively use their enforcement powers.

Predatory Pricing

Enacted in 1890, the Sherman Act makes it illegal to monopolize or attempt to monopolize commerce. The courts have long interpreted the Sherman Act to prohibit predatory pricing, "the deliberate sacrifice of present revenues for the purpose of driving rivals out of the market and then recouping the losses through higher profits earned in the absence of competition."[5]

An aggressive competitor lowers prices as a result of greater efficiencies and astute management. A predator, by contrast, lowers prices to eliminate competition and reap the rewards of a dominant market position. The precise point where aggressive price competition becomes predation is not always clear. Fearful of inhibiting genuine competition, the courts have grown increasingly cautious in dealing with claims of predatory pricing. In 1993 the U.S. Supreme Court issued a landmark decision that established a very high standard of proof for predatory pricing cases.

In that case, which involved a cigarette manufacturer accused by a competitor of predatory pricing (Brooke Group Ltd. v. Brown & Williamson Tobacco Corp. (1993), 113 S. Ct. 2578), the Court held that a plaintiff must provide evidence that the defendant priced goods below actual costs for a sustained period of time with an intent to injure competition and that the defendant had a dangerous probability of actually driving competitors out of business and recouping the losses incurred in below-cost pricing through future profits gained in a monopoly market. Although the Court found that the evidence of the defendant's anticompetitive intent "more voluminous and detailed than any other reported case," the plaintiff was unable to meet the difficult challenge of proving the defendant capable of attaining a monopoly position and recouping losses in the future.[6]

The Supreme Court concluded in Brooke Group that "predatory pricing schemes are rarely tried, and even more rarely successful." The FTC and the Department of Justice agree and have been cautious in pursuing complaints of predatory conduct. Yet recent scholarship has suggested that predatory pricing may be more common than previously believed.[7] Certainly many independent retailers feel that they have been victims of predation, but the high standard of proof makes successful legal action a monumental task. Some have even suggested that the Court's decision in Brooke Group may prove "fatal to all future predatory pricing claims."[8]

Price Discrimination

Although the focus on retaining a decentralized economy of many small producers and merchants has largely faded from the interpretation of antitrust law, this earlier intent is embodied in the language of the Robinson-Patman Act.

Passed in 1936, the law was created at a time when Americans were alarmed at the rapid expansion of chain stores. Between 1926 and 1933, the portion of total retail sales captured by chain stores grew from 9 percent to 25 percent.[9] Congress believed that these large firms could gain unfair advantages by using their market power to demand price discounts from manufacturers and suppliers that were unavailable to small merchants. According to Donald Clark of the FTC, the Congressional "purpose behind the Robinson-Patman Act was to provide some measure of protection to small independent retailers and their independent suppliers from what was thought to be unfair competition from vertically integrated, multi-location chain stores."[10]

The Robinson-Patman Act is actually an amendment to Section 2 of the Clayton Act, which was enacted in 1914 as the first federal statute that expressly prohibited certain forms of price discrimination. Section 2 barred price differences only when their effect "may be substantially to lessen competition or tend to create a monopoly in any line of commerce." In 1936, the Robinson-Patman Act amended this section, making it illegal to:

> discriminate in price between different purchasers of commodities of like grade and quality . . . where the effect of such discrimination may be substantially to lessen competition or tend to create a monopoly in any line of commerce, or to injure, destroy, or

prevent competition with any person who either grants or knowingly receives the benefit of such discrimination, or with the customers of either of them.

The Robinson-Patman Act bars manufacturers and other suppliers from discriminating in price and makes it illegal for buyers such as retail merchants to induce price discounts not made available to other purchasers. Quantity discounts are allowed only to the extent that they reflect actual differences in the supplier's cost of manufacture, sale, or delivery of goods. The law, as elaborated by the FTC Act, prohibits sellers and buyers from using brokerages, allowances, and other services to accomplish price discrimination indirectly. The Robinson-Patman Act differs from the original Clayton Act in that, in addition to prohibiting price discrimination that harms market competition in general, it also forbids discrimination that injures an individual competitor.

Both the Department of Justice and the FTC are charged with enforcement. Injured businesses may bring private lawsuits under the act as well.

The courts have made certain violations of the law subject to the same stringent interpretation and standard of proof as is required of predatory pricing claims under the Sherman Act. Known as "primary line" cases, these involve injury to competition between the seller granting the discriminatory discount and other sellers. In Brooke Group, the Supreme Court held that primary line injury under Robinson-Patman is of the same general character as the injury inflicted by predatory pricing schemes and is therefore subject to the same standard.

The other type of case brought under the Robinson-Patman Act, known as "secondary line" injury, occurs when competition is harmed between favored buyers—those receiving a lower price—and disfavored buyers. In retail, this would apply if a manufacturer or supplier sold the same product to different retailers at different prices with the effect of the injuring competition.

In secondary line cases, there is a decade-old split in the Circuit Courts yet to be settled by the Supreme Court as to whether a plaintiff must prove that the discriminatory pricing harmed competition in general, rather than simply providing evidence of harm to a particular competitor.[11] That is, if competition in a given market remains healthy, does discriminatory pricing that injures a particular competitor constitute a violation?

Historically the answer was yes—Robinson-Patman was enacted to ensure that a small business was not at a competitive disadvantage by virtue of its size—but a 1988 ruling by the D.C. Circuit Court attempted to undo the original intent of law by finding that if competition in a relevant market remained vigorous, no violation had occurred.

It was far from being a firm judicial stance; three different opinions were issued in the case. A stinging dissent came from Judge Abner Mikva, who insisted that Congress had intended to protect small businesses by creating a simpler standard for proving competitive injury: "Congress was convinced that, by protecting small businesses, it was also protecting the operation of a competitive economy."[12]

In the years following this decision, four Circuit Courts have dealt with secondary line cases, and Mikva's view has prevailed in all four. Most recently, in 1997 the 9th Circuit ruled that "injury to competition in a secondary-line Robinson-Patman case is conclusively established by proof of injury to a competitor." The history and language of the law, the court concluded, evinced a "Congressional intent to protect individual competitors, not just market competition, from the effects of price discrimination."[13]

The Robinson-Patman Act has fallen into disfavor with many antitrust scholars and enforcers, who view its focus on ensuring a decentralized economy and protecting individual competitors rather than consumer welfare as inconsistent with the appropriate role of antitrust policy. Some have called for its repeal, arguing that using market power to pressure suppliers for special deals is a legitimate business strategy and one that often produces lower prices.

The Justice Department has declined to enforce Robinson-Patman during the last thirty years, leaving prosecution of illegal price discrimination entirely to the FTC, which itself has been reluctant to pursue alleged violations. During the 1980s, both agencies came close to formally requesting that Congress repeal the statute.[14]

Booksellers Challenge Superstore Tactics

In March 1998 a group of independent booksellers together with the American Booksellers Association, which represents 3,500 bookstores, filed a lawsuit in northern California against Barnes & Noble and Borders Books, alleging violations of the Robinson-Patman Act, the California Unfair Trade Practices Act and the California Unfair Competition Law (state statutes will be discussed in more detail below).

The lawsuit accuses the book chains of using their market power to engage "in a pattern and practice of soliciting, inducing, and receiving secret, discriminatory, and illegal terms from publishers and distributors," unavailable to independent booksellers.[15] The illegal terms include discounts not available on the published pricing schedule, discounts on small orders that were not given to independent booksellers ordering the same volume, and special pricing for new chain outlets. The suit also accuses the chain stores of soliciting and receiving special deals from publishers for advertising or prominently displaying particular titles.

Borders and Barnes & Noble are representative of the growing power of corporate chains relative to both their independent rivals and their suppliers. With combined sales of $5 billion in 1997, the two chains are larger than the top ten publishers combined.[16] This makes publishers vulnerable to demands for special deals and discounts. "We're scared of them. If they don't like our terms of sale, they threaten not to buy our books," contends one publishing executive.[17] Especially concerned are the independent publishers, who historically have relied on small booksellers to promote titles that may have literary merit but, without a well-known author or large promotional spending, are of little interest to the chains.

Antitrust violations have a long history in the book industry. In 1979, the FTC launched an investigation into whether publishers were favoring chain stores over independents with special prices and promotional fees. The investigation proceeded at a snail's pace. In 1988, the FTC issued six administrative complaints against publishers Harper & Row, Hearst, Macmillan, Putnam Berkley, Random House, and Simon & Schuster for violations of the Robinson-Patman Act and the FTC Act.

The complaints detailed a variety of discriminatory pricing practices, and also noted that the nation's three largest bookstore chains at the time—Waldenbooks (now owned by Borders), B. Dalton (now owned by Barnes & Noble), and Crown Books—were the recipients of the favorable terms. Included in the complaints were allegations that the chains received unjustifiable volume discounts and special pricing not shown on published schedules and paid a lower price per book than the independent bookstores, even on orders of equivalent size. The publishers were also accused of making promotional, display, and inventory control services available only to the chains. The publishers in turn maintained that the discounts were cost-justified; for instance, they argued, sales staff only needed to visit one corporate office rather than many independent stores.[18]

Consent agreements were reached with each of the six publishers in 1992. The terms of the deals were not made public, and the FTC put the matter on hold for further evaluation. In September 1996 the FTC dropped its investigation, rejected the consent agreements, and dismissed the complaints, citing "significant developments that have occurred in the industry since the complaints were issued—including the initiation of private litigation addressing many of the same issues."[19]

Tired of waiting for the FTC to address illegal practices in the book industry, the ABA, along with six independent bookstores, filed a federal antitrust lawsuit against five publishers in May 1994. The publishers—Houghton Mifflin Company, Penguin USA, Rutledge Hill Press, St. Martin's

Press, and Hugh Lauter Levin Associates—were accused of violating Robinson-Patman by granting unfair and illegally preferential volume discounts and promotional allowances to national book chains and warehouse buying clubs.[20] In January 1996 the ABA filed a separate case against Random House, the largest trade publisher.

By June 1997 the ABA had reached settlements with all six publishers, representing at that time about 40 percent of the industry. The consent orders provided for flatter pricing schedules and proportional access to promotional money. The publishers covered legal expenses, but the ABA did not seek further damages. In September 1997 Penguin USA was found to have violated the terms of the deal—to the tune of $170 million in illegal discounts and allowances given to the chains—and paid the ABA $25 million.[21]

At issue in the current suit against Barnes & Noble and Borders are both unfair discounts and special deals on promotional and advertising expenses, commonly referred to as "co-op payments." Examples of size of these payments were provided by *Publishers Weekly* in 1997. Books-A-Million, a regional chain store that is significantly smaller than its two large rivals and likely receives smaller co-op fees, earned $750 per month for placing a book in the "New & Notable" section, $3,000 for placing it the Christmas catalog, $7,500 for store employees to read and promote the book, and $12,000 for the company president's stamp of approval. By contrast, a large independent might receive $50 for displaying a book at the front of the store. Most independent booksellers are too small for publishers to bother with.[22]

Returns are another issue in the lawsuit. Publishers typically provide discounts and promotional fees based on the volume of books purchased. The ABA complaint charges that the chains "often massively overbought and undersold titles." A study by Open Book Publishing found that the return rate for national chains is approximately 50 percent higher than the return rate for the average independent bookstore and some estimates suggest that the chain stores return as much as 40 percent of their purchases. This practice creates inefficiencies and headaches for publishers who report returns of new hardcover books in 1996 ran between 35 and 50 percent, compared with 15 to 25 percent ten years ago.[23] Discounts and promotional fees are not returned along with books, placing small stores that buy at appropriate volumes at a disadvantage.

The ABA contends that Barnes & Noble and Borders have been engaged in anticompetitive practices since the late 1980s or early 1990s and that the market saturation strategies of the two chains are "being fueled in significant part by secret and illegal terms" and much of this expansion "can only be profitable if the chains receive illegal deals and existing independent booksellers are driven out of the marketplace."[24]

The long-term result will be detrimental to consumers. What books are published and distributed will depend on the decisions of a few centralized buyers, and the discounts that have drawn consumers into chain stores will become less necessary as competition dries up. Already, according to the ABA, both chains now "sell the majority of their books at no discount."[25]

The lawsuit seeks an end to anticompetitive practices, recovery of legal fees, and damages. "We believe if we have a relatively level playing field that we'll survive," says David Unowsky, owner of The Hungry Mind, a locally owned, independent bookstore in St. Paul, Minnesota. "But if they conspire to run us out of business, very few independents will be able to survive."[26]

Independent Video Stores May Follow Suit

Independent video retailers may follow the booksellers' lead. The Independent Video Retailers Group (IVRG), formed in 1998, is considering an antitrust lawsuit against the major movie studios and Blockbuster Video, which currently captures 30 percent of all video rental sales.[27]

IVRG contends that Blockbuster, whose parent company, Viacom, owns one of the major movie studios, Paramount Pictures, is receiving unfair deals from the studios that are unavailable to independent video stores. Blockbuster has negotiated deals directly with the studios to purchase videos at $6 each, rather than the industry average of $65. Under a revenue-sharing plan, the chain keeps 60 percent of rental income and gives the rest to the studios. Revenue-sharing has been around in some form for about a decade, but according to the independents, the traditional formula that they work under provides 55 percent for the studios, 5 percent for the distributor that handles the account, and only 40 percent for the retail outlet.[28] Perhaps representing an ominous new trend for independent stores, Blockbuster recently signed a deal with three film companies, giving it exclusive rights to 45 movies.[29]

State Antitrust Laws

About 24 states prohibit pricing products below cost with an intent to injure competition.[30] Usually known as Unfair Trade or Practices Acts, most of these statutes were enacted during the 1930s and, like the Robinson-Patman Act, reflect an earlier understanding of the purpose of antitrust policy and an attempt to stem the tide of small business failure. Because of this history, state unfair trade acts take a fundamentally different approach to predatory pricing than federal law, often providing a simpler standard for establishing a violation.[31]

Under the 1937 Arkansas Unfair Practices Act, for instance, businesses may not sell a good or service "at less than the cost thereof to the vendor . . . for the purpose of injuring competitors and destroying competition." The Wisconsin Unfair Sales Act states that the "practice of selling certain items of merchandise below cost in order to attract patronage is generally . . . an unfair method of competition in commerce." In California, it is "unlawful for any person engaged in business within [California] to sell any article or product at less than the cost thereof to such a vendor, or to give away any article or product, for the purpose of injuring competitors or destroying competition."[32]

While federal courts impose a heavy evidentiary burden in predatory pricing cases, requiring evidence that the defendant had a dangerous probability of monopolizing the market and recouping its losses, most state statutes provide a simpler standard, focusing on evidence of below-cost sales and a predator's intent to harm rivals. In many cases, intent to injure competitors may be inferred directly from the extent and duration of below-cost sales. One state, Louisiana, prohibits retail sales below cost regardless of the seller's intent or the effect of such sales.[33]

A few states do not allow private citizens to take legal action under unfair trade laws, but where the opportunity exists, independent businesses might succeed in obtaining relief from a corporate competitor whose loss leaders seem aimed directly at their livelihood. In November 1994 Home Depot was accused of violating Utah's Unfair Trade Practices Act by selling building supplies below cost. It was not the first time the home improvement giant's pricing practices were questioned. In Georgia, a painting contractor noticed that Home Depot's prices in Atlanta, where the chain dominated sales of building supplies, were substantially higher than in Augusta and Savannah, where it still faced competitors. According to the painter, a year's worth of supplies would run his business $2,500 more in Atlanta than elsewhere.[34]

The suit in Utah was filed by a local chain, Standard Plumbing Company, which operated 14 building supply stores. Although refusing to admit wrongdoing, Home Depot quickly agreed to an out of court settlement and ceased selling items below cost.[35]

Community Pharmacists vs. Wal-Mart

In November 1993 a chancery court in Faulkner County, Arkansas, ruled that Wal-Mart had violated the state's Unfair Practices Act by pricing a substantial portion of its pharmacy goods below cost with an intent to injure three independent pharmacists. It was the first case ever tried under the 1937 statute. In addition to the shock of a successful lawsuit against the nation's largest retailer—carried out in its home state no less—the ruling came just four months after the U.S. Supreme Court adopted the stringent predatory pricing standard in Brooke Group and generated sudden interest in state unfair trade laws as a viable legal option for small businesses facing predatory competitors. Two years later, however, a divided Arkansas Supreme Court reversed the chancery court decision on appeal.

Wal-Mart had been selling up to 30 percent of its pharmaceutical and health and beauty aids below its acquisition costs, a point never contested by the retailer. The lower court inferred an intent to injure competition based on the number and frequency of below-cost sales, the extent of such sales, the retailer's stated policy to "meet or beat the competition without regard to cost," in-store price comparisons made by Wal-Mart employees of products sold at other stores, and the disparity between prices in Faulkner County and other markets with more and less competition.[36]

The Arkansas Supreme Court rejected the lower court's decision by a four to three vote. The Court concluded that loss leaders were not illegal and the fact that Wal-Mart would regularly sell various pharmaceutical items below cost was not sufficient to infer a violation of state law. Such an inference would require a "sustained effort to destroy competition in one article by selling below cost over a prolonged period of time." The Court stated that in-store price comparisons aided competition and could not be used to infer anticompetitive intent. Continued profits at the independent pharmacies and the presence of other discount retail chains in the area were also a factor in the ruling.[37]

Many observers applauded the Arkansas decision as bringing state law into alignment with federal antitrust policy. Though the language of state unfair trade laws offers a more attainable standard for plaintiffs in predatory pricing cases, the Arkansas Supreme Court's decision may indicate that state courts are following federal courts in taking a more restrictive view of what constitutes anticompetitive behavior. Given the seemingly diminished chances of success and the expense of litigation, few independent retailers will consider this option worthwhile.

The changing dynamics in the retail industry, notably the growing market power of chain stores and the shifting balance of power between retailers and manufacturers, warrant closer inspection by antitrust authorities. Local merchants will face an increasingly tenuous existence if their giant competitors are allowed to tilt the playing field to their own advantage while antitrust enforcement remains passive and no longer infused with a civic concern for decentralizing ownership.

In the meantime, many communities are taking matters into their own hands, enacting rules at the local level to defend their homegrown economies.

CHAPTER four

Planning and Zoning for Healthy Main Streets

In hundreds of towns across the country, local residents have turned once quiet planning board meetings into centers of noisy democracy in an effort to save their towns from corporate retailers. In Greenfield, Massachusetts, a group of citizens secured a ballot referendum to overturn the town's zoning decision to allow development of a Wal-Mart store. After an intense grassroots campaign, the citizens group won the vote and kept the retailer out. In Gig Harbor, Washington, 14,000 people signed petitions to halt the arrival of Wal-Mart and hundreds turned out at public hearings to voice their opposition. The giant retailer finally withdrew its plans. "Never believe that money will win over what's good for a community. . . People are learning that small towns need to defend themselves against large corporations, and we have proved that can be done," said one resident.[1]

In Plymouth, Massachusetts, a massive year-long community effort to stop a 135,000 square foot Home Depot led the town's planning board to reject the superstore's request for a special permit. Residents of the North Beach neighborhood of San Francisco faced down a 9,000 square foot Rite Aid pharmacy with a petition signed by 8,000 and a billboard that read, "Rite Aid, Wrong Place." A public forum recently held in Decorah, Iowa, in response to Wal-Mart's plans to build a supercenter on the edge of town drew more than 500 people.

"I smile when I see those big crowds," says Lee Snyder, a Washington Township trustee, "because it helps us know what we should be doing." Citizen protest in Snyder's small Ohio town led Target to drop its plans for a large discount department store. Stories like these have been repeated many times over. Sprawl-Busters, a group that helps communities organize to stop corporate retail development, counts more than sixty successful campaigns in the last few years alone.[2]

Preventing a corporate retailer from setting up shop in one's community is a formidable task. Citizens face well-financed marketing campaigns, lobbyists, and media relations specialists, and, more often than not, municipal officials swayed by promises of new jobs and tax revenues. Many communities are caught off guard by the arrival of a corporate chain and have little time to react. Chain stores typically keep the specifics of their expansion plans to themselves. Often these retailers work for an entire year or more with local developers, who assist in purchasing a site, planning the development, and preparing zoning applications, and all the while keep local residents in the dark about the site's intended user. After a zoning application is submitted, the municipality may only have a set few weeks to review the proposal. If officials approve the development and a citizens' group opts to challenge the decision through a referendum, they can expect to be severely outspent in the campaign. Wal-Mart spent nearly $100,000, or 25 times as much as its opponents, to win a ballot measure in Fort Collins, Colorado. Home Depot spent $440,000 on a similar initiative in Toledo, Ohio.[3]

Worse still, many communities determined to prevent corporate retail development are thwarted by their own planning and zoning laws. Certain areas may be zoned for large-scale retail development ("as-of-right" zoning) with no opportunity for citizens or municipal officials to review and reject development proposals. Comprehensive planning is altogether absent in many places. Other towns have plans and zoning codes that are decades old, crafted long before the expansion of corporate retail chains and ill-equipped to protect a town's character and local economy.

Such was the case in Westlake, Ohio. In 1993, residents were shocked to discover that Kmart owned a 32-acre site locked into a quiet residential area. The site had been zoned three decades earlier for a shopping center, and Kmart's plans for a 190,000 square foot, 24-hour grocery and discount department store were well underway. Because the zoning code allowed for this type of development, Westlake was forced into four years of expensive legal battles with Kmart. National retailers do not hesitate to challenge local land use decisions in the courts. Fighting back can be a long and costly endeavor, prompting many communities to simply give in. Westlake chose not to, and did finally prevail in court, but just barely and only after being able to provide convincing documentation that the town had intended the area for neighborhood-serving stores, rather than a large-scale store of regional impact.[4]

Rather than being left to the mercy of retail developers, many communities are revising local zoning rules with an eye towards protecting their cities and towns from corporate retail development. Communities have substantial power over local land use and zoning policy. Courts have consistently granted local governments considerable leeway to exercise this authority to preserve the vitality of the central business district and the physical and commercial character of the community. Increasing numbers of communities are using this authority to enact rules that defend local businesses and encourage a homegrown retail economy.

Examples of these rules are provided below and are intended as a starting point for communities concerned about the expansion of national retailers. One size doesn't fit all, however, and land use rules should be crafted to meet the particular needs and goals of a community. Many of the examples here are from small towns. Urban areas present more complex challenges, but can be approached on a neighborhood by neighborhood basis with rules fashioned to meet the circumstances of each area. Some communities, for instance, may decide that local merchants and large-scale retailers can successfully coexist so long as the large stores are restricted to downtown and barred from sprawling into outlying neighborhoods. The essential point is that cities and towns are not at the mercy of retail developers, but can use land use policy to nurture a retail and service economy that benefits community.

The Comprehensive Plan

There are two primary pieces of local land use policy: the comprehensive plan, which is essentially a vision statement containing general guidelines for development, and the zoning code, which implements the plan through concrete rules governing land use.

A number of communities have included in their comprehensive plan an intention to preserve and strengthen local businesses, limit commercial development to downtown or other existing retail districts, and restrict the proliferation of corporate chain stores.

In the North Beach neighborhood of San Francisco, for instance, "small-scale, neighborhood-serving businesses are strongly encouraged."[5] The Local Comprehensive Plan for Kent County, Maryland, lists among its objectives "support [for] small, locally owned businesses" and "prevent [tion of] commercial sprawl outside the county's existing traditional commercial centers."[6]

The comprehensive plan for Skaneateles, New York,

states, "Rather than establishing competing shopping centers in the Town to provide basic goods and services, the Village commercial center (which has been the traditional focus of retail sales) should remain the center for shopping in the community."[7]

Following an invasion of name-brand "outlet" stores that drove out a number of local businesses, citizens of Manchester, Vermont, adopted a new Town Plan that calls for the town to "create and maintain a business environment which is hospitable to locally-owned and managed businesses. . ." and "create regulations which will serve to moderate the increased presence of retail businesses" that promote "nationally- or regionally-known brand name(s) to attract a non-resident customer base" and have "a well-recognized identity in many other communities, and thus [their] presence in Manchester would tend to detract from the Town's uniqueness or distinctiveness as a place to visit."[8]

Strong comprehensive plans yield a number of important benefits. In addition to serving as the basis of zoning codes, plans provide land use officials with guidelines for reviewing development permits and applications to rezone certain sites. Plans that clearly articulate a policy to promote small, local retail businesses and discourage corporate chains will help ensure that these community goals are the focus of planning board decisions.

Comprehensive plans give municipalities legal protection if a particular land use decision is challenged in court. Generally, cities and towns have been granted broad control over local land use policy, provided that zoning rules and decisions reflect legitimate public purposes, are reasonable and fair, and are not arbitrary and capricious. Land use decisions that flow rationally from goals outlined in a comprehensive plan demonstrate an adherence to the interest of public welfare rather than arbitrary or unequal treatment of a particular land owner or developer.[9]

For citizens seeking to prevent a particular development, demonstrating that the development is at odds with the comprehensive plan can be a powerful argument with local officials. In some states, land use decisions are required by law to conform to local plans. If a city council or planning board succumbs to pressure from a corporate retailer requesting a special permit or rezoning of a site, a comprehensive plan will give citizens a powerful weapon for challenging that decision in a referendum or through the courts.

In many states, municipalities can enact a moratorium on commercial development while they prepare a local plan or revise zoning laws, provided that the moratorium promotes valid public purposes, is limited in duration, and is used for planning.[10] In 1994, after several large chains announced plans to locate in Fort Collins, Colorado, the city council enacted a six-month moratorium on all retail construction larger than 80,000 square feet to allow the community time to consider the impact of superstores and plan accordingly.[11] Similarly, the tiny village of Williamsville, New York, placed a six-month ban on construction in 1997 after rumors that Walgreen was eyeing a location on Main Street. Williamsville used the time to revise its 15-year-old town plan.[12]

Zoning Rules

A municipal zoning ordinance defines what type of development is appropriate in each area of the town or city, as well as the restrictions and special conditions that govern development. A number of communities have fashioned creative zoning rules to limit chain store development and encourage a more rooted retail and service economy. [13]

Limiting Size

More than half of all new retail space in the U.S. in recent years has come in the form of superstores or "big boxes."[14] Not counting their vast parking lots, these massive retail outlets range from 90,000 to 250,000 square feet, two to five times the size of a football field and 20 to 50 times the size of a typical downtown retailer. New stores of this magnitude almost certainly lead to significant sales losses and potential failures at dozens of existing businesses. Moreover, these sprawling, monolithic structures place tremendous burdens on public infrastructure—a single superstore can generate as many as 20,000 car trips daily—and are at odds with the compact, walkable neighborhoods that many communities prefer.

A number of cities and towns have responded to this problem by restricting the size of new retail stores. Though not new, size caps have become more common in the last few years as communities grapple with the expansion of superstores and seek ways of protecting their homegrown businesses and the unique character of their cities and towns.

In the United States size caps are currently limited to municipal zoning, but other countries, such as France, have enacted size caps on a national level. Most recently, Ireland blocked the development of stores larger than 32,100 square feet (3,000 meters), citing concern for the environment and small merchants. The interim measure was enacted in 1998 and will remain in effect pending a governmental review of the impacts of superstores.[15]

Examples of Size Caps:

Skaneateles, New York After three consecutive six-month building moratoria in response to a proposal to construct a 150,000 square foot shopping center, this small town of 7,500 people developed a comprehensive town plan and enacted a zoning restriction limiting retail stores to no more than 45,000 square feet and shopping center sites to no more than 15 acres.[16] "We try very hard here to maintain the idea of small shops," said Town Attorney James Murphy. "If someone like a Walgreen's comes in, they'll put the little hardware guy out of business and significantly change the character of Skaneateles."[17]

Westford, Massachusetts In 1993, Wal-Mart walked away from plans to build in this town after intense opposition from residents. Determined not to be caught off guard again, Westford adopted a town plan, banned retail stores larger than 60,000 square feet, and provided for a more thorough review and special permitting process for stores between 30,000 and 60,000 square feet.[18]

North Elba (Village of Lake Placid), New York Wal-Mart finally dropped its plans for a store in North Elba in October 1998 after a five-year battle with residents that included filing three lawsuits against town officials, all of which the retailer lost. The ordeal prompted the community to enact a size ordinance limiting single retail stores to 40,000 square feet and capping shopping centers at 68,000 square feet.[19]

Tolland, Connecticut After launching a successful grass-roots campaign against a 50-acre superstore development, the citizens of Tolland set a size limit of 52,000 square feet on retail businesses.[20]

Wilton, Connecticut Wilton placed a 30,000 square foot cap on retail businesses. Stores over 20,000 square feet are required to conduct traffic and economic studies to assess the store's impact on neighborhood streets and the town's central business district.[21]

Roswell, Georgia Prompted by Target's plans to build a 176,000 square foot store in this suburb of Atlanta, the Roswell city council revised its zoning code in August 1997, prohibiting retail stores larger than 100,000 square feet.[22]

Clermont, Florida In April 1999 Clermont became the first town in Florida to cap the size of retail developments. The new law bans stores larger than 100,000 square feet and was adopted in response to Wal-Mart's plans to build a 200,000 square foot outlet in Lake County.[23]

Rather than placing outright bans on stores over a certain size, a number of towns have set size thresholds beyond which developers must apply for special permits, allowing for citizen input and review by planning boards.

Plymouth, Massachusetts Plymouth's zoning bylaw requires a special permit for stores larger than 6,000 square feet. Approval depends on the support of four out of five members of the Zoning Board of Appeals. In 1991 the village of Cedarville, a part of Plymouth that has been targeted by big box stores including Home Depot, adopted a rule prohibiting commercial buildings larger than 24,000 square feet.[24]

Greenfield, Massachusetts Stores that are larger than 20,000 square feet or that generate more than 500 car trips per day are considered to be major developments warranting special review. Applicants are required to submit a number of impact analyses covering traffic, environmental, community, and fiscal concerns.[25]

Mill Valley, California The town's zoning law requires stores larger than 1,500 square feet to apply for a special use permit. The requirement stalled a proposed 6,250 square foot Blockbuster Video store for months, and the developer ultimately withdrew its plans.[26]

Size caps have been upheld by the courts as a valid use of local authority. Most recently, in a March 1998 decision, the Ohio Supreme Court upheld the village of Chardon's ordinance limiting businesses in a certain commercial zone to no more than 10,000 square feet or 10 employees. The Court refused to hear the appeal of a developer who contended the ordinance violated property rights and was unconstitutional.[27]

Assessing Community Impact

The weakness of municipal zoning restrictions in the age of the automobile is that corporate retailers denied approval in one community may well find acceptance in an adjacent town. Many corporate retailers are large enough to have an economic impact beyond municipal borders, and the town that declined the development may find itself not only lacking the tax revenue generated by the new store, but with a threatened local economy as well. Although citizens finally convinced Wal-Mart to scrap its plans for North Elba, the retailer is now investigating a location ten miles away in a neighboring village.[28]

Regional cooperation offers a solution to this problem. A handful of regions have taken this approach, creating joint planning agencies charged with reviewing applications for developments that exceed a certain size, or developments of regional impact (DRIs).[29]

The Cape Cod Commission One of the most effective is the Cape Cod Commission, established in 1990 by Cape Cod voters concerned about the impact of rapid growth on the character of their communities. This regional planning agency has the authority to approve or reject proposals for new construction larger than 10,000 square feet and changes of use for commercial sites that exceed 40,000 square feet.

The review process involves a public hearing and focuses on the project's impact on the environment, traffic, community character, and local economy. Applicants bear the burden of demonstrating that the project's benefits outweigh its detriments, and that the development is consistent with the goals of regional and local comprehensive plans.[30]

Cape Cod's regional policy plan, which provides the Commission with guidelines for reviewing development applications, states that, when reviewing a project, the Commission "should take into account any negative impacts that the project would have on the Cape Cod economy and should encourage businesses that are locally-owned and that employ Cape Cod residents."[31]

The Regional Policy Plan also expresses concern for the diversity and unique character of the region:

> Retail sprawl in general is inefficient and unsustainable. The standardized architecture and corporate signage tend to detract from Cape Cod's unique regional character. The surplus of retail operations both locally and nationally indicates that over-retailing

does not add to the region's economic pie. It ends up hurting smaller, locally-owned businesses and creating blight when existing retail buildings are vacated.[32]

Unlike many cities and towns, the Cape Cod Commission has concluded that nurturing existing small enterprises and encouraging homegrown development is often a more effective long-term economic strategy than recruiting expanding companies. The Commission works closely with the Cape Cod Economic Development Council, which provides technical support and counseling for small businesses, and the Lower Cape Cod Community Development Corporation, which has established a revolving small business loan fund.

Armed with a regional land use plan and careful review of large-scale developments, Cape Cod residents have given a number of corporate retailers the cold shoulder. The Cape Cod Commission rejected Wal-Mart's plans to locate in Falmouth in 1993. Sam's Club met the same fate in Hyannis that year as well.

In 1994, the Commission denied a permit for a 120,000 square foot Costco wholesale club in the town of Sandwich, concluding that the project was inconsistent with the regional plan's goal of sustainable development and would have adverse impacts on environmental resources, community character, and local businesses. Costco filed suit in Barnstable County Superior Court, challenging both the decision and the constitutionality of the Commission itself. The retailer, however, eventually dropped its lawsuit.[33]

More recently, Home Depot applied for a permit to locate in Yarmouth. Strong local opposition, combined with the powers of the Cape Cod Commission, led the corporation to back away from its project in March 1997.[34]

The Commission's focus on preserving existing businesses and blocking large corporate retailers has created some controversy, but a 1995 survey of Cape Cod residents indicated that the Commission's actions have been consistent with community objectives. Residents opposed a "large discount wholesale or retail store" by a nearly two to one margin. Sixty-five percent said they did not support a "nationally advertised fast food chain," and 92 percent favored reusing existing sites for development rather than expanding into new areas.[35]

Vermont's Act 250 Vermont pioneered a cooperative approach to large-scale development on a statewide level in 1970 with Act 250, which arose in response to the arrival of Vermont's first interstate highway in the late 1960s. Residents feared that the highway would lead to rapid, uncontrolled growth and ultimately the destruction of the state's rural character and picturesque towns.

Act 250 requires developments of regional impact to obtain a land use permit from the one of the state's district environmental commissions. In most cases, commercial developments require Act 250 review when they encompass ten or more acres of land, a threshold substantially higher than under Cape Cod's rules. Act 250 approval depends on meeting several conditions that focus on the project's environmental and economic impact. Decisions by the state's nine district environmental commissions may be appealed to the state Environmental Board and ultimately the Vermont Supreme Court. Members of the district commissions and the state board are appointed by the governor.[36]

In addition to the law's environmental criteria concerning water and air pollution, energy conservation, and soil erosion, Act 250 specifies that developments must not place unreasonable fiscal burdens on the ability of local governments to provide education and other services, must not exhaust the town's ability to accommodate growth, and must be consistent with local land use policies. Act 250 discourages scattered development by requiring a project to be contiguous to existing settlements unless the tax revenue generated by the development exceeds the additional cost of public services required by the project. Act 250 also considers a development's impact on scenic and historic sites.[37]

Act 250 has limited the number of large-scale retailers in Vermont. The state was the last U.S. frontier for Wal-

Mart, which built its first store there in 1995. Vermont now has four Wal-Mart stores, but as a result of Act 250, three of these are about half the size of a typical Wal-Mart and were located in existing buildings. In Bennington, Wal-Mart opened a 52,000 square foot store in a former Woolworth's building, and, in Rutland, a 75,000 square foot store was located downtown. Most recently, Wal-Mart opened a 66,000 square foot store in Berlin. The store occupies a building that previously housed another department store.[38]

With the aid of Act 250, residents successfully fought Wal-Mart's plans to open a 100,000 to 126,000 square foot store on the fringes of the economically depressed town of St. Albans. The legal controversy spanned several years, finally landing in the Vermont Supreme Court, which upheld the Environmental Board's decision against Wal-Mart's proposal on the basis that the store would harm local businesses, weaken the local tax base, and reduce funding for public services.[39]

Favoring "Community-Serving" Retail

Corporate retailers, particularly large-scale stores, often draw consumers from a wide area, inundating neighborhoods with traffic and pollution and diminishing the quality of life and property values of nearby residents. An invasion of national retailers may also drive up commercial rents, making survival difficult for smaller merchants that sell basic daily goods to neighborhood residents. The town of Manchester, Vermont, for instance, has suffered from a proliferation of name-brand "outlet" stores that primarily serve the area's tourists. The outlet stores have caused commercial rents to escalate, forcing out businesses like hardware and variety stores that serve local residents.[40]

Palm Beach, Florida, has crafted a unique ordinance to address this problem. This island community, determined that its commercial district should be humanly scaled and serve the needs of local residents, has converted its main commercial district into a "town-serving zone." Establishments in the zone must be smaller than 2,000 square feet and must primarily serve "town persons," those living, visiting, or working in Palm Beach. Businesses larger than 2,000 square feet may apply for a special permit provided that they can "satisfy the council that not less than 50 percent of the anticipated customers will be 'town persons'" rather than shoppers from the mainland.[41] The ordinance was upheld in a 1991 court case in which the judge concluded that the restriction served legitimate public interests and reflected the community's desire to "limit displacement of businesses serving the Worth Avenue neighborhood by larger, regional establishments."[42]

Demanding Diversity

As corporate businesses displace local merchants, America's towns are becoming marked by a stark uniformity. Thanks to a creative local ordinance, this is not the case in Carmel, California. In the mid-1980s, Carmel became the first town to outlaw formula restaurants, defined in the zoning code as food service businesses "required by contractual or other arrangements to offer standardized menus, ingredients, food preparation, employee uniforms, interior decor, signage or exterior design," or "adopts a name, appearance or food presentation format which causes it to be substantially identical to another restaurant regardless of ownership or location." In short, the rule banned chain restaurants.[43]

Since then several communities have followed Carmel's lead. In 1989 Bainbridge Island, Washington, adopted a zoning ordinance banning formula restaurants. "We struggle with how we can legally keep our island from becoming Anyplace, USA," remarked then-Mayor Alice Tawresey.[44]

Solvang, California, a 100-year-old village famous for its Danish architecture, enacted a formula restaurant ban in 1994. The ordinance reads, "The Village Area is unique not only because of its Danish architecture, but because of its small individualized shops and restaurants. . . This unique character would be adversely affected by a proliferation of 'formula restaurants' which are required by contractual or other arrangements to be virtually identical to restaurants in other communities. . ."[45]

In 1995 Pacific Grove, a town noted for its 1880s architecture and located on the northern tip of the Monterey Peninsula in California, prohibited formula restaurants.[46] So too did Sanibel Island, Florida in 1996. According to David Tolliver of the Sanibel Chamber of Commerce, the ordinance "balances the best interests of the business community and private citizens' enjoyment of the island's unique ambiance."[47]

To date, no community has enacted a ban on formula retail establishments, though Solvang did consider such a measure in 1995 when concerns were mounting over the proliferation of "outlet" shopping centers. "A lot of visitors expressed disappointment that our little, unique Danish village was turning into corporate America," said one Solvang resident.[48] The town appointed a task force to study lowering the town's 3 percent cap on commercial growth and banning formula retail businesses. The task force defined a formula retail business as "a single-source, high traffic retailer operated directly by, or under contract with, a manufacturer of the merchandise offered for sale therein, and required to adopt standardized layout, decor, uniforms, or similar standardized features."[49]

Ultimately, the majority of the task force opted to maintain the status quo on growth and not to prohibit formula retailers. Two of the nine committee members voting on the formula retail restriction disagreed with the majority's opinion, arguing that "the majority has failed to convince us that Solvang's local regulations are sufficient to protect its residents and merchants from a recent phenomena in the displacement of independent, locally owned businesses by national and international retail moguls."[50]

One of the minority's main concerns was the loss of diverse, independent local businesses that had demonstrated a "tenacity for weathering economic ups and downs." The minority argued that formula retail in the setting of a tiny village was an inefficient use of fixed resources:

> Many of Solvang's current, independent retail businesses offer a variety of products under one roof. By definition, most formula retail businesses offer one type or make of merchandise (e.g., underwear, shoes, leather items, etc.). The net result is that more resources in the form of space are required by a larger number of formula retailers to offer access to the same variety of products.[51]

One of the main arguments made by the majority was that formula retail businesses generate more sales tax revenue per square foot compared to Solvang's independent retailers ($1.88 vs. $0.99 between 1991 and 1994).[52] The minority disputed this finding:

> Firstly, it fails to account for the fact that—unlike most independent retailers—formula retailers rely heavily upon off-site warehousing and office space. However, off-site office and warehouse space was not factored into any of the majority's calculations. Secondly, it does not account for lost local reinvestment when replacing locally owned independent retailers with formula retailers, including revenues to neighboring support businesses (e.g., local accountants, insurers, contractors, etc.), charities and community involvements.[53]

The minority also made the point that sales tax accounts for only 25 percent of Solvang's revenue. Property tax, the fastest growing source of revenue, accounts for 21 percent, and the transient occupancy tax collected from hotels represents 30 percent. The minority questioned the impact that uncontrolled chain retail development would have on property values and the number of visitors who come to Solvang, suggesting that while formula retail may offer an efficient short-term source of revenue, the loss of uniqueness could adversely affect more important long-term revenue streams.[54]

Though never enacted, the language Solvang considered to deter corporate retailers provides a useful model for others to follow.

Losing local businesses to national chains stores is by no means inevitable. Indeed, the growth of chain stores has been aided in no small part by public policy. Land use rules have all too often ignored the needs of communities and undermined the stability of existing business districts. Development incentives frequently favor national corporations over locally owned businesses. Increasing numbers of communities are rewriting the rules around a different set of priorities that encourage a homegrown economy of humanly scaled, diverse, neighborhood-serving businesses. As the examples above indicate, active decisionmaking at the local level and a creative approach to zoning can provide a powerful arsenal for defending community.

For citizens seeking resources, strategies, and assistance in building a constituency and changing local zoning policies, the appendix provides a listing of organizations that can help. A number of these organizations have pioneered other useful strategies for revitalizing Main Street, which can be combined with the policy approaches provided here.

CHAPTER five

Taxing Chain Stores

Although potent tools for encouraging a homegrown economy, zoning ordinances cannot be used to ban developments on the basis of ownership; that is, communities cannot legally exclude absentee-owned retail and service businesses. They may, however, use local ownership —as the Cape Cod Commission has done—as one factor in deciding whether to grant a permit to a new business.

Communities may also have the authority to impose special taxes on absentee-owned stores. Such taxes were once fairly common.

When the first wave of chain store expansion hit the U.S. in the years following World War I, it met with vigorous opposition. Although chain stores had been around for many decades, they did not become a significant force in American retailing until the 1920s. At the turn of the century, chain stores accounted for only 3 percent of retail sales. By 1926, the chain store segment of total retail sales had reached 9 percent and from there expanded rapidly, capturing more than one-quarter of all sales by 1933. The growing market share of chain stores was most pronounced in gas and grocery sales. In 1933, chain stores accounted for more than one-third of total gas sales and 44 percent of grocery sales.[1]

The Great Atlantic and Pacific Tea Company (A & P) exemplified the new breed of retailers. The company grew from 200 stores in 1900 to more than 15,000 outlets by 1929. With revenues exceeding $1 billion, A & P was capturing more than 11 percent of all grocery sales. Other large chains of the period included J.C. Penny with 1,452 stores, F.W. Woolworth with 1,881 outlets, and Montgomery Ward with 556 stores.[2]

As chain stores gained momentum, so too did concerns about their impact on communities. By the late 1920s, the "chain store problem" had entered national political debate in full force. Unlike the narrow focus on efficiency and consumer welfare that dominates today's discussions of corporate retailers, Americans in the 1920s and 1930s were primarily concerned with community. Opponents of the chain store system argued that absentee ownership was draining local economies, threatening the civic fabric of the nation, and undermining democracy by concentrating economic power and transforming a nation of independent merchants into a nation of clerks.[3]

Many politicians agreed. "A wild craze for efficiency in production, sale, and distribution has swept over the land, increasing the number of unemployed, building up a caste system, dangerous to any government," said Senator Hugo L. Black of Alabama. "Chain groceries, chain dry-goods stores, chain clothing stores, here today and merged tomorrow. . . The local man and merchant is passing and his community loses his contribution to local affairs as an independent thinker and executive."[4]

Organized resistance to the expansion of the chains began in the 1920s when independent merchants and their suppliers boycotted manufacturers who sold directly to the chain stores. The effort proved unsuccessful, and the anti-chain store movement sought other avenues of relief. Some independent merchants formed cooperatives in an effort to achieve the economies of scale and buying power afforded to the chains. By 1936, cooperatives operated more than 500 retail stores.[5]

Others fought for legislation to restrict corporate retail expansion. At their annual meeting in 1922, the National Association of Retail Grocers (NARG) suggested that the number of chain outlets allowed in a community be limited by law. Realizing that such legislation would probably not be able to withstand constitutional challenge, NARG changed tactics and began pushing for new taxes on chain stores that would increase according to the number of outlets operated by a chain.[6]

In 1927, Georgia, Maryland, and North Carolina became the first states to enact chain store taxes. The new laws, however, were overturned by the courts. A breakthrough came in 1931, when the U.S. Supreme Court upheld Indiana's 1929 chain tax law by a five to four vote. Indiana's tax was collected as an annual fee for business licenses and ranged from $3 for the first store to $25 per store for 20 or more outlets. The appellant in the court case owned a chain of 225 groceries and argued that the $5,443 tax bill he faced denied him equal protection under the 14th Amendment of the U.S. Constitution.[7]

The Supreme Court determined that the distinction between chains and independents was reasonable enough to justify separate tax classifications. The Court would go on to uphold chain store tax laws on a number of occasions, including New Jersey's in 1935 and Louisiana's in 1937.[8]

In all, between 1927 and 1941, 28 states passed chain store tax bills. Most were challenged in the courts, but 22 survived.[9] The taxes usually took the form of a graduated license or occupation tax levied annually. Their severity varied greatly. In Montana, for instance, the top rate was a mild $30, reached on the eleventh store. Texas was more aggressive, assessing $750 per store for systems with more than fifty outlets.[10] Pennsylvania levied $500 per store in chains exceeding 500 units.[11] Iowa collected both a per store tax ($155 for chains with more than fifty units) and a gross receipts tax of 10 percent on earnings above $1 million.[12] Most states counted only the stores within their borders. The exception—Louisiana—based its tax on the number of outlets a chain operated nationally, collecting $550 per in-state store belonging to systems with more than 500 units.[13]

Economic historians still debate the impact of these taxes on chain store expansion. The effect in states that assessed very mild taxes of around $30 per store was likely minimal. On the other end, the $750 per store tax in Texas could absorb a substantial chunk of profits. This was particularly true for grocery store chains, which operated the most outlets and also had very low profit margins. In 1929, the average net profit per store in the grocery business was $1,694, compared to $3,242 for shoe stores, $7,841 for drug stores, and $16,237 for variety stores.[14] The Depression pushed margins even lower: by 1935, the net profit for grocery stores had fallen to $950.[15] The disparity in profit margins between different types of stores meant that, in 1932, Woolworth, a variety store chain, paid 1 percent of its net profits in chain store taxes while Kroger Grocery and Baking Company paid 40 percent.[16]

One way or another, the share of retail sales captured by chain stores dropped from 27.0 percent in 1933 to 24.5 percent in 1935 and 22.8 percent in 1939. The chain store segment of the retail market would remain just below 23 percent throughout the 1940s. Grocery chains, which accounted for about a third of all chain store sales, led the decline, falling from 44 percent in 1933 to under 37 percent by the end of the decade.[17]

One of the unintended consequence of chain store taxes was the rapid adoption of franchising as a distribution method among petroleum companies. When Iowa imposed a tax of $155 per station plus 10 percent of gross receipts over $1 million in 1935, Indiana Standard Oil Company began discontinuing its retail operations in the state and instead leased stations to independent dealers. Much to the company's surprise, this system proved to be very successful and generated immediate increases in sales. By 1937, Indiana Standard had handed over all of its company-operated stations to independent dealers. Though limited primarily to gas stations in this period, franchising was well on its way to becoming a major force in the U.S. economy.[18]

In addition to chain store taxes, independent retailers were making legislative progress on other fronts as well. The National Association of Retail Druggists (NARD) successfully lobbied for state fair trade practices laws. Eventually, 45 states enacted some form of fair trade legislation, 20 of which chose to adopt NARD's model language. Many of these laws legalized resale price maintenance agreements between manufacturers and retailers, which helped ensure that small retailers' prices were not undercut by their larger competitors. In 1937, the Miller-Tydings Act exempted resale price maintenance agreements from federal antitrust laws.[19]

In 1935, the Wholesale Grocer Association, whose members depended on independent grocers, helped draft the legislation that ultimately became the Robinson-Patman Act. Sponsored in the House by Representative Wright Patman, who insisted that "there is no place for chain stores in the American system," the original law was much tougher on chain stores than the final version enacted in 1936. It did not include, for instance, the meeting competition defense, which allows for price discrimination in order to meet a competitor's price.[20]

Despite the passage of the Robinson-Patman Act, 1936 marked the beginning of the end for the anti-chain movement. With the grocers in the lead, the chain stores mounted a massive campaign that included advertisements, speakers, radio broadcasts, and political lobbying. Their arguments are familiar to us today. The community-building aspects of independent retail stores—local ownership, dispersed wealth, charity and civic contributions—were considered, at most, secondary functions. Retail's primary purpose was to benefit consumers through wide selection and low prices, and in this, the chains argued, they were tremendously successful.[21]

In 1936, a chain store tax proposal in California was defeated by referendum. A & P was instrumental in the proposal's defeat, enlisting the support of farmers by absorbing a bumper crop of produce without depressing prices. Organized labor—a severe critic of chain stores as recently as 1937—became an ally when A & P signed a series of collective bargaining agreements in 1938 and 1939.[22] A chain tax referendum failed in Utah in 1941.

At the national level, Congressman Patman drafted legislation for a national chain store tax in 1938, but his bill died in the House Ways and Means Committee after A & P spent $500,000 to defeat it.[23] Patman made another unsuccessful attempt in 1940. The national tax would have dealt a death blow to many of the chains. The bill levied a $50 tax on stores in chains with 9 to 15 units and escalated to $1,000 per store in chains of more than 500 units. Companies were then required to multiply this tax by the number of states in which they operated.[24] The bill was designed to be phased in over a period of years to allow large, multistate chains time to sell a portion of their stores.[25] Had the tax been in effect in 1938, A & P would have owed $472 million in taxes with earnings of only about $9 million.[26]

No new chain store taxes were enacted after 1941. Most of the existing taxes were repealed. Some were left on the books, but ultimately rendered insignificant by inflation.[27]

Perhaps the time has come to dust off this old idea and once again favor local over absentee ownership. Cities or states could adopt progressive license fees to do business within their borders; these fees would increase according to the number of stores operated by a company. Already certain kinds of businesses are exempt or pay reduced license fees in many places. These are usually businesses connected to the public good, such as doctors' offices. Communities have every reason to expand this notion of public good to include an ownership criteria.

A progressive license fee could be improved over the original chain store taxes by tying it more closely to the physical size of stores. Many historians agree that chain store taxes were one of a number of factors, including the automobile, pushing companies to open ever-larger stores. Supermarkets, for instance, first appeared in the grocery business during the 1930s.[28] Ideally, a progressive license fee would account for both the number of outlets and the total square footage operated by a chain.

CHAPTER six

Restoring Franchise Autonomy

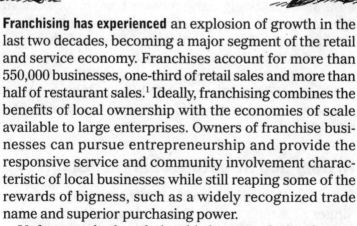

Franchising has experienced an explosion of growth in the last two decades, becoming a major segment of the retail and service economy. Franchises account for more than 550,000 businesses, one-third of retail sales and more than half of restaurant sales.[1] Ideally, franchising combines the benefits of local ownership with the economies of scale available to large enterprises. Owners of franchise businesses can pursue entrepreneurship and provide the responsive service and community involvement characteristic of local businesses while still reaping some of the rewards of bigness, such as a widely recognized trade name and superior purchasing power.

Unfortunately, the relationship between the local entrepreneur (the franchisee) and the company marketing the product or service (the franchisor) is often marked by a great disparity in power. Governing this relationship is the franchise contract. Over the last 15 years contracts have grown increasingly one-sided, transferring obligations and risks to the franchisee and rights and rewards to the franchisor. Much of this shift in control has been made possible by the high demand for franchises and, ultimately, the relentlessly promoted, though false, perception that franchises are more likely to succeed than independent businesses.

Today many franchisees operate as mere extensions of the franchise corporation, not as independent businesses owners. Franchisors exert unilateral control over many aspects of the enterprise. They are often able to terminate the contract at their discretion or restrict the sale of the business, making it difficult for franchisees to receive fair market value for their investment. While franchise contracts vary from one system to the next, in the worst cases, franchisees have traded a lifetime of savings for a risky investment and a low-paying job with long hours and little autonomy. Prospective franchisees are often unaware of these problems. The federal government and most states offer them little in the way of basic protections.

In the early 1990s, franchisees responded to the growing abuse within the industry by forming trade associations to collectively bargain with franchisors and to demand legislative action. They sought new rules at both the state and federal level that would set minimum standards of fair dealing, bar the worst abuses of franchisor power and ensure a more equitable franchise relationship. Their efforts met with success in Iowa in 1992, but franchisors were able to stop action in other states and at the federal level.

History and Structure of Franchising

Many date the beginning of franchising to 1851, when the Singer Sewing Machine Company brought itself back from the brink of financial disaster by converting its sales representatives to independent dealers. The dealers purchased Singer's sewing machines up front and retailed them in exclusive territories granted by the company.[2] This kind of arrangement constitutes a "product and trade name" franchise, which involves a network of licensed dealers who distribute a manufacturer's product under an identifying trademark. Despite its early start, this form of distribution did not get underway in earnest until the 1920s and 1930s when both automobile and petroleum companies, lacking the capital necessary to establish a system of company-owned outlets, sought other ways of rapidly penetrating the market.

Under the other form of franchising—"business format franchising"—the franchisor is selling an entire business concept, including a product or service, trade name, methods of operation, and building design. Businesses like McDonald's and Speedy Oil Change are part of this category. Though some of these franchise systems trace their origins to the 1920s, it was the 1950s and 1960s that brought an explosion of business format franchising, aided in part by an increasingly mobile society.

Business format franchises surpassed product and trade name franchises in total numbers during the 1980s. Currently, they account for 77 percent of all franchise businesses. Product and trade name franchises, however, generate more than two-thirds of all franchise revenue.[3] On average, about 20 percent of the units in a franchise system are owned and operated by the franchisor. This ratio has remained steady for the last twenty years.[4]

The average start-up investment required of a franchisee is $143,000, but may range from a few thousand dollars to a few million dollars depending on the business.[5] Launching a McDonald's, for instance, costs more than $500,000. A 7-11 convenience store requires about $13,000. Costs for hotels are in the millions. This start-up investment includes an initial fee of between $2,000 and $60,000 paid to the franchisor. In some systems, the franchisee owns the site, building and equipment. In others, the outlet is leased from the company. The franchisor collects annual royalty payments that range from 3 percent to 50 percent of gross revenue.[6] An 8 percent royalty is common. Franchisors also collect regular payments to fund advertising and marketing, usually as a percentage of annual revenue, and may require franchisees to purchase supplies exclusively from the franchisor or its affiliates.

From the franchisor's perspective, one of the primary benefits of franchising is that it allows a company to expand rapidly without the capital expenditures required to own and operate all of the outlets. In addition, the company reduces its risk of failure to the extent that the investment capital is supplied by the franchisees. Franchisors also benefit from having their outlets run by people who have a substantial stake in the success of the business and who can respond to the needs of the local customer base in ways no absentee owner could.

Forty years ago, franchisees were truly independent business owners. In exchange for their investment, franchisees were granted the right to market the franchisor's product and trademark for a given period of time over an exclusive territory. They gained the advantages of a proven product or business concept with a well-established trade name, and operated in partnership and with the support of the franchisor. This enabled them to avoid many of the costly errors inherent in new business ventures. When the contract came to an end, franchisees could continue their business as independents, retaining the value and goodwill built into the business through their investments and labor.[7]

Franchising: A Risky Investment?

What was once a fairly equitable arrangement has since evolved into a business relationship characterized by a serious imbalance of power. In the last ten years, franchise contracts have grown from about ten pages to more than fifty as franchisors incorporate every possible protection and financial advantage available to them while stripping the franchisee of their autonomy and traditional rights, often including their ability to seek legal recourse in the event of a conflict.[8]

Some argue that a franchisee's ability to negotiate the contract provides sufficient protection against abuses. Franchise contracts, however, are typically offered on a take-it-or-leave-it basis with no room for negotiation. The most popular franchises have long waiting lists (20,000 are in line for a McDonald's), enabling franchisors to establish terms as they please. Franchise salespeople are adept at presenting the franchisor as an able guardian of the franchisee's interests, despite the fact that the financial interests of both parties are often at odds. Prospective franchisees lack the information and the top-notch legal advice available to franchisors. The reasons that many people decide to buy a franchise—lack of business training or experience—may make them especially vulnerable to accepting a contract that does not protect their interests.

What few prospective franchisees in this situation realize is that they are not entering into a partnership to distribute a product or expand a business. The product being sold is the franchise itself.[9] Although there are certainly franchisors with long-term growth strategies that are committed to the actual product or service being offered to consumers and to the health of their network of outlets, all too often people buy into a franchise system in which the franchisor generates little revenue from royalties (as a result of failing franchise outlets), but instead earns the bulk of its income from the sale of new franchises.

The high demand for franchise businesses and the one-sided contracts that franchisors are able to exact is in large part a result of the widespread belief that franchise businesses rarely fail. Franchisors have relentlessly promoted this idea and the federal government has failed to offer reliable data on the true survival rates of franchises. Figures widely disseminated by the International Franchise Association (IFA), a trade group of franchisors, indicate that 1 percent of franchisees fail in their first year, 5 percent after five years, and 10 percent over a decade. This is compared to a 80-82 percent ten-year failure rate given for independent businesses. The IFA cites the Department of Commerce and the Small Business Administration as the source of these figures. Congressional and academic researchers, however, have not been able to locate these statistics in the reports of either agency.[10]

Despite repeated calls for action at hearings held in 1992, the federal government has failed to challenge these fraudulent claims and to supply reliable information on the success of franchises. The Commerce Department stopped collecting data on franchising in 1987. The Department's data prior to that year does not give figures for franchise failure rates. It does, however, indicate that between 1972 and 1987, 44 percent of all *franchisors* went out of business. This certainly begs the question of what happened to the franchisees in these systems? Other evidence collected since 1987 has shown similarly high rates of failure among franchisors.[11]

To date, the most comprehensive study of franchisee survival rates was done by Dr. Timothy Bates of Wayne State University on behalf of the Small Business Administration. The study tracked small independent and franchise businesses started in 1986 or 1987 until 1991. Although the franchise firms were better capitalized than the independents, the study found that 62 percent of the franchises survived versus 68 percent of the independent businesses. Profits were much higher for the independent businesses while, on average, the franchisees actually registered a loss.[12]

Industry observers have concurred with these figures. In 1991, Rupurt Barkoff, then chairman of the American Bar Association's Forum on Franchising, estimated that for the typical franchise system, "probably at best a third are doing very well, a third are in definite financial trouble, and a third maybe break even."[13]

When franchisees fail, the public hardly notices. Franchise businesses are rarely seen boarded-up or being torn down, because franchisors often sell the same failing franchise outlet repeatedly. "Churning," as this process is known, not only prevents the appearance of failure but each sale generates new revenue for the franchisor. Typically a failing franchise is taken over by the franchisor and stripped of its supplies and equipment. The business is not sold as a going concern—that is, the new buyer never sees the books kept by the previous owner—but is instead presented with regional sales figures. The entering franchisee may also fail and the procedure begins anew.[14]

The perception of franchising as an almost risk-free investment sustains both the large, well-known franchise systems and thousands of new, smaller systems. Many people interested in investing in a franchise discover that the most popular franchise systems have long waiting lists and high start-up costs. They may instead opt for one of many new "bargain" franchise opportunities. These franchisors often lack the proven track record, recognized trade name, support and national marketing capabilities that makes franchising attractive in the first place.

One-Sided Contracts

What follows are the major provisions common in franchise agreements that fail to protect a franchisee's investment and that can lead to abusive behavior by franchisors.

Termination Most franchise contracts contain provisions that allow the franchisor to terminate the relationship at any time. Though the agreement may outline specific causes for termination, such as failure to comply with procedures in the operating manual, the number and detail of such obligations enables franchisors to find fault with almost any franchisee. This threat of termination, and with it the potential loss of the franchisee's investment and livelihood, can be used by franchisors to coerce behavior or impose unreasonable conditions on franchisees.

Nonrenewal Contracts last from five to twenty years and may contain periodic options to renew. The term renewal, however, is misleading. At the time of renewal, the franchisee is presented with a new contract that may include terms substantially different from those in the original agreement, such as higher royalty fees or new obligations. Franchisees' reluctance to forfeit years of work and financial investment, as well contract restrictions on selling the business or going independent (discussed below), force many to accept unreasonable renewal terms.[15]

Baskin Robbins franchisees currently seeking renewal, for instance, are being told that they must invest $200,000 to convert their stores to combined Baskin Robbins-Dunkin Donuts outlets. The two companies merged and believe combination stores will be well received by the market, but the risks of this experiment are being shouldered by the franchisees.[16]

Transfer The ability to sell the business and obtain a fair market value—the ultimate measure of ownership—is frequently subject to unreasonable restrictions. Most contracts require the franchisor to approve any new owner prior to a sale. This protects the franchisor's good name and trade mark and ensures that the buyer meets its qualifications. However, these clauses are often abused. The franchisor may require that the prospective buyer accept a new contract rather than assume the existing contract. If the terms of the new agreement are less advantageous, then the franchisee will face a reduced selling price.

Franchisors have also used their right of first refusal on a blanket basis as a means of preempting the sale of the business altogether. Prospective buyers, aware that they are likely to be refused by the franchisor, will not bother to make an offer. The only buyer left is the franchisor itself and the end result is the sale of the business at less than fair market value. One trade association of franchisees all belonging to the same system estimated that this practice over a two-year period resulted in a net loss of equity on the part of the system's franchisees of more than $1.5 billion.[17]

Without the power to sell the business, the franchise contract grants little more than the opportunity to earn a profit over a fixed period of time. The appreciated investment may not be fully recoverable. Successful franchisees are especially vulnerable to transfer restrictions and abuses as the franchisor may wish to acquire and operate the most profitable outlets itself.

Encroachment The next best thing to acquiring a profitable outlet is to locate a new one nearby. Encroachment—when franchisors grant new franchises or build company-owned stores that cannibalize the sales of an existing outlet—is perhaps the most immediate threat to a franchisee's profit margin and equity. For decades, the granting of a defined territory to a franchisee was a core element of the contract and an essential part of making a profit. With the exception of certain businesses, such as auto dealerships or bottling companies, franchise contracts no longer provide for a guaranteed territory. More recently, following a number of lawsuits over encroachment (rarely won by franchisees but costly for franchisors), contracts specifically state that the franchisor has the right to open an outlet anywhere.

Franchisors are not subject to the same market controls that the owner of a chain of stores would be in considering the decision to open a new outlet. An individual who owns a chain of stores must balance the potential sales from a new outlet against the potential losses at his or her existing outlets. A new unit will only be worthwhile for the owner if established outlets remain profitable. For a franchisor, new franchises mean additional fees and any increase in sales generates new royalties even if this forces another outlet's margin so low as to not be worthwhile to the franchisee.

Though perhaps permitted by the contract, encroachment certainly represents a violation of the franchisee's expectations at the time of the agreement and can have a profound effect on the profitability and value of the investment.[18]

Sourcing Although franchising should provide small business owners with greater purchasing power and thereby reduced costs, often any savings that result from improved economies of scale accrue only to the franchisor. Many franchise agreements mandate that franchisees purchase supplies and equipment from the franchisor, its affiliates, or designated vendors, often at higher prices than the franchisee could obtain elsewhere.

In one popular national restaurant chain, franchisees are required to purchase supplies exclusively from the franchisor. Half of the franchisor's income is generated from these sales, but at an estimated cost of $10,000 annually to each franchisee over the price of comparable goods.[19] In exchange for a captive market, kickbacks and commissions often accompany deals between franchisors and vendors not directly affiliated with them.

While franchisors clearly have a stake in ensuring that supplies meet appropriate standards, this need can be met—as some franchisors have done—by establishing strict product specifications, but allowing franchisees to select vendors.

Non-Compete Clauses Franchise contracts almost always contain post-termination clauses that bar the franchisee from engaging in a similar business over a period of years. This effectively destroys the sweat equity and good will built up by franchisees and prevents them from continuing in their chosen field. The physical business they have purchased is often only suitable to that particular activity and upon termination they will face the problems outlined earlier of attempting to sell the business at fair market value. Frequently, terminated franchisees end up rapidly liquidating their assets at fire sale prices and losing the going concern value built into their establishments. Non-compete covenants make franchisees extremely vulnerable to accepting unfair renewal contracts.

Legal Rights Franchise agreements may require franchisees to waive their legal rights under certain federal and state statutes. Often they also require that any litigation be conducted in the franchisor's home state under the laws of that state. More recently, franchise contracts have stipulated that all conflicts must be arbitrated, usually at the franchisor's corporate headquarters.

The Limits of Disclosure

There are two broad areas in which legislation can protect the interests of franchisees: rules that govern the sale of franchises, known as disclosure or registration laws, and rules that set minimum standards of behavior for the ongoing relationship between franchisees and franchisors, known as relationship laws.

With the exception of a couple of specific industries within franchising, the federal government has concentrated its efforts on disclosure. During the late 1960s and early 1970s, a large number of public complaints, class action lawsuits, and business failures led state and federal governments to scrutinize the rapidly expanding enterprise of franchising. Congressional hearings concluded that much of the problem originated with misrepresentations and fraudulent claims made by franchisors prior to making a sale. FTC investigations during the 1970s concurred, finding "widespread evidence of deceptive and unfair practices" in franchise solicitations. State attorneys general estimated losses to consumers from franchise fraud in the millions of dollars.[20]

In response, a number of states as well as the federal government established rules requiring the pre-contract disclosure of information relative to the franchise business. California was the first to do so with its 1970 Franchise Investment Act. Fifteen other states have since enacted their own disclosure rules.[21] In 1979, the FTC created a national franchise disclosure rule.[22]

Meeting both state and federal disclosure requirements can usually be accomplished by presenting the prospective franchisee with a Uniform Franchise Offering Circular (UFOC), which details some two dozen pieces of information such as the financial standing of the franchisor and the number of outlets in the system. Under the state laws, franchisors must register the UFOC with the state where it is kept on file and possibly reviewed. Franchisors are not required to submit their offering circulars to the FTC.

Many complaints have been raised regarding the FTC rule. Franchisee advocates argue that the rule gives the appearance of government regulation of franchise sales when in fact the rule is only minimally enforced. The few state disclosure laws do provide for a private right of action (the ability of private individual or entity, as opposed to a government agency, to take legal action under a given law), but no such right exists at the federal level. During the initial drafting of the rule, the FTC recognized that a private right of action would be necessary for effective enforcement, but this right was never incorporated into the rule's language and the courts have consistently interpreted no such right to exist.[23]

Enforcement, then, has been left entirely to the FTC, which has been both understaffed and reluctant to use its authority. Between 1979 and 1994, the FTC filed 60 lawsuits under the disclosure rule. Critics contend that this effort is far too meager for an industry that generated 1,363 complaints to the FTC between 1990 and 1992 alone.[24] Franchisees who make complaints to the FTC have been told that the agency only pursues alleged violations involving a large number of franchisees in the same system.[25] As a result, "franchisors have been able to commit random violations of FTC guidelines with relative impunity."[26]

Restoring the Rights of Small Business Owners

By the late 1980s and early 1990s, unfair practices and misuse of power had become so rampant in franchising that thousands of franchisees organized two national trade associations, formed organizations within their respective chains, and demanded new legislation to restore their rights as business owners.

The movement reached a crescendo in Iowa in 1992, when franchisees, led initially by disgruntled members of the KFC system and soon joined by others in chains from Dairy Queen to Jiffy Lube, succeeded in convincing the Iowa Legislature that new rules were needed. The state passed a comprehensive franchise relationship law on April 2, 1992. Committee hearings had convinced both Democrats and Republicans that Iowa's franchisees were being taken advantage of. The final vote in the House was 87 to 11; the Senate voted 40 to 5.[27] Republican House Representative Joseph M. Kremer summed up the feeling: "It's my opinion the business in Iowa should not be dictated to by these large international conglomerates."[28]

Franchisors immediately mounted a massive campaign to overturn the legislation, declaring Iowa's law a threat to the future of franchising and predicting a decline in the state's economic growth. Amendments in 1995 altered some of the act's provisions, but the "Franchisee Bill of Rights," as it is known, has remained largely intact.

Although franchisors have claimed the Iowa legislation to be unprecedented in its stringency, a number of its provisions can be found elsewhere. About one-third of the states have laws that govern some aspect of the franchise relationship. In addition, almost every state regulates automobile dealerships, gasoline stations, liquor distributors, and farm implement dealers.[29]

Common provisions in state laws covering franchises are rules that require good cause for termination or nonrenewal, meaning that a franchisor's decisions in this area must be based on legitimate business reasons and cannot be arbitrary or capricious. Occasionally state laws prohibit restrictions on sourcing except in the case of goods trade marked by the franchisor.[30] Most bar franchise contracts from requiring franchisees to waive their rights under the law.

Some state statutes are very weak or narrow in scope. The franchise statute in Arkansas, for instance, applies only to franchises in systems not covered by the FTC disclosure rule (those franchisors with less than $15 million in annual sales).[31] Few franchises meet this standard. Other states offer stronger protections. Wisconsin's law, for instance, bars termination, nonrenewal and substantial changes to the competitive circumstances of a contract without good cause. It also provides for a 60-day period in which franchisees have the opportunity to correct deficiencies prior to being terminated.[32]

Nevertheless, Iowa's law is unique both in its comprehensive approach and its timing. It was the first franchise law enacted in more than a decade.[33] A number of its provisions are not found in other states with franchise relationship laws.

The statute's encroachment section was perhaps the most controversial. In its initial form, the act barred the establishment of new outlets within an "unreasonable proximity" of an existing franchise, unless the franchisor offered a right of first refusal to the affected franchisee or compensation for the lost market share. The law defined an "unreasonable proximity" for food franchises as the smaller of a three-mile radius or an area incorporating 30,000 people. For nonfood franchises, the law did not define unreasonable proximity.[34]

In 1995, amendments to the Iowa law weakened the encroachment section. Rather than banning encroachment outright, the statute now allows franchisees to seek damages in court if the franchisor fails to offer a right of first refusal, does not provide compensation for lost sales, and the total impact of the new outlet exceeds 5 percent of the existing franchisee's annual revenue.[35]

Iowa's franchise law also allows franchisees to sell their businesses, provided that the new franchisee meets the franchisor's "reasonable current qualifications." Franchisors may not require the new owner to enter into a new contract if time remains on the original contract. Franchisees may pass the business to an heir upon death or disability with no restrictions.[36]

The law prohibits the enforcement of non-compete clauses upon termination or nonrenewal of the franchise, unless the new business relies on a "substantially similar marketing program" as the franchise or unless the franchisor offers to purchase the franchisee's assets at fair market value.[37] In addition, the statute bars restrictions on sourcing, allowing franchisees to select vendors for all supplies and equipment excluding products tied directly to the franchisor's trademark.[38]

Like other states, Iowa requires good cause for termination or nonrenewal. In the case of termination, a franchisor must provide the franchisee with written notification of a problem and allow 30 to 90 days for correction before the contract may be terminated.[39] The law prevents contracts from requiring franchisees to waive rights under the statute, voids all contract provisions that prevent litigation from being held in the franchisee's state, and provides for a private right of action.

Initially the Iowa Franchise Act was retroactive, but this was overturned by a 1993 lawsuit brought by Holiday Inn and McDonald's. Only franchise contracts entered into after the statute's passage are subject to its terms.[40] Since 1992, 20 states have considered franchise legislation, but franchisors successfully prevented any of these laws from passing.[41]

Following the enactment of Iowa's law, a number of franchisors boycotted the state and the IFA predicted the law would injure the state's economy. According the American Franchisee Association, however, franchisors continued to open outlets in Iowa, including those that had declared a boycott.[42] To date, there is no reliable evidence to suggest that the act has affected the number of new franchise outlets in the state. Some analysts insist that these laws encourage the health and expansion of franchising by providing reasonable investment protection and ensuring an optimal allocation of risks and rewards.[43]

In addition to a sharp decline in the number of new franchises in Iowa, the IFA predicted that more franchisors would opt to open company-owned outlets rather than franchises and thereby limit opportunities for local ownership. There is no evidence that this has occurred in Iowa.[44] A 1991 study examined this concern in regard to states that regulate franchise termination. The researchers found that in nonrepeat-customer industries, such as hotels and fast-food businesses, there was a slight difference in the number of company-owned versus franchised outlets in states with and without regulations. In regulated states, there was a 77.6 percent chance that a new unit would be franchised compared to an 80.1 percent chance in without regulation. For repeat-customer industries, such as home cleaning services, there was no difference in the number of company-owned versus franchised outlets.[45]

Relationship Laws at the Federal Level

Half of the states have neither disclosure nor relationship laws (except for specific industries such as auto dealers or gas stations), and another six only regulate pre-sale disclosure. In these states, franchisees who feel they have been misled, abused, or otherwise taken advantage of have no legal recourse except that provided by common-law contract rules, such as alleging that a franchisor breached the implied duty of good faith and fair dealing. Here, courts defer to the content of the contract, and, because franchisors have tried to incorporate every conceivable protection in their contracts, franchisees have had very little success in seeking redress under common-law principles.[46]

In response to the lack of adequate state regulations and to set a minimum standard for fair franchise relationships, hearings have been held and legislation introduced in Congress throughout the 1990s. Federal legislation was endorsed by the 1995 White House Conference on Small Business, which declared, "Congress must remove the barriers that prevent franchisees, dealers, and product distributors from exercising their basic legal and constitutional rights..."

Over the years several different bills have been introduced in Congress. The most recent, HR 4841, was introduced in late 1998 and is expected to be reintroduced in 1999. Its ten sponsors include both Democrats and Republicans.

Titled "The Small Business Franchise Act," HR 4841 would prohibit sourcing restrictions, non-compete clauses, and termination without good cause. It bars unreasonable restrictions on the sale of franchises, allowing franchisees to transfer the business to people who meet the franchisor's current, reasonable standards for new franchisees. The act would prohibit franchisors from locating new outlets in an unreasonable proximity to existing franchises, defined as near enough to reduce the existing outlet's sales by five percent or more in the first year. Of great importance—considering the failure of federal enforcement of disclosure rules—is the bill's authorization of private legal action and actions undertaken by state attorneys general on behalf of state residents.

Precedent exists for a federal franchise relationship law. During a time when gasoline stations and car dealerships dominated the industry, Congress recognized the need for regulation and enacted two laws designed to protect franchisees in these sectors: the Automobile Dealers Franchise Act of 1956 and the Federal Petroleum Marketing Practices Act of 1968.[47] Though both laws are fairly weak, offering only general standards of behavior, they do acknowledge the need for good faith conduct in franchising, prohibit termination without good cause, and provide for a private right of action.[48] The franchisees covered by these federal laws now constitute only a fraction of all franchises.

The U.S. Small Business Administration has considered adopting lending rules requiring that franchisees be granted a certain level of autonomy in order for them to qualify for the SBA's small business loan program. The SBA, which backs up to 80 percent of the value of low-interest loans to small businesses, is barred by law from assisting large companies. Franchises, which account for about 10 percent ($979 million in 1996) of the SBA's assistance, pose a dilemma.[49] "If a franchisor imposes so much control upon a franchisee that a franchisee is not an independent operator but just a branch of the franchisor, then we are not able to assist in that franchise business," explains Ronald Matzner, the SBA's associate deputy general counsel.[50]

As a result, SBA officials review each applicant's contract to verify that the franchisee has been granted sufficient autonomy to be considered a genuine small business owner. The agency, for instance, will not assist 7-11 convenience store franchisees, because each store must deposit all revenue to a central account that is controlled by the franchisor.[51] In 1996, the SBA proposed defining specific lending rules and adding new standards that franchisors would need to meet for their franchisees to qualify for SBA loans, notably a requirement that franchisees be granted a defined territory.[52] Franchisors fought the proposal and the SBA backed down.

The lack of general franchise relationship laws in most states and at the federal level has meant that the majority of franchisees lack appropriate protections to ensure their legal rights and financial interests. Legislation is needed to establish minimum standards of fair conduct and equitable distribution of risks and rewards, and to balance and protect the interests of both franchisees and franchisors. New rules are needed to reestablish franchisees as true business owners and prevent franchises from becoming predominantly controlled by large corporations located far from the communities these businesses serve.

Ideally, federal legislation would provide minimum national standards for fair franchising, while allowing states to retain the right to enact stronger protections and to provide enforcement. Legislation has been proposed that would do this. The SBA should revisit its proposal to enact stricter requirements for franchisees under its lending program. Most new franchises require loans, many of which are backed by the SBA. Codified minimum standards would foster more equitable franchise agreements. At the state level, Iowa's law provides a good model, perhaps with the original encroachment provisions reinserted. Another model could be found in the SBA's proposal: states could require that franchise contracts include a defined territory, within which encroachment would be prohibited.

CHAPTER seven

Expanding Cooperatives

Many franchisees derive little benefit from their affiliation with large corporations. Franchisees lack autonomy, are more likely to fail than independent businesses, and reap little of the financial rewards of improved economies of scale. Given this, perhaps a better option for local merchants seeking the advantages of scale would be to join a purchasing or wholesale cooperative. These cooperatives are owned by retail businesses. Decisionmaking is shared and profits are funneled back to members.

Retailer-owned purchasing and wholesale cooperatives have experienced a burst of growth in the last ten years as independent businesses look for ways to remain competitive with national retailers. Cooperatives give small merchants greater purchasing power, enabling them to lower the cost of goods through volume buying, and, like national retail companies, purchasing coops are often able to negotiate directly with manufacturers. TruServ, a wholesale hardware cooperative, reduces merchandise costs for its members by 10 to 20 percent.[1]

Some retailer-owned cooperatives serve only as a buying group. Others operate warehouse and distribution facilities for their members, an important role considering that many distributors have been squeezed out of the market by national retailers. Many coops provide members with additional advantages that normally would be unaffordable to independent businesses, including national advertising, brand identity, and expert marketing and business advice. Many have taken an aggressive stance towards competition from national retailers by setting up loan funds and providing consultants to help their members update their stores, install new technology, and streamline operations.

Little data is available on the success of independent businesses that are members of purchasing or wholesale cooperatives, but by all accounts most are faring better than their unaffiliated counterparts.[2] In the hardware industry, where cooperatives date back nearly a century, the number of independent stores has fallen about 12 percent since the mid-1970s, but this still amounts to a much smaller decline than has occurred in other independent sectors.[3]

Competition from chain stores prompted many formerly unaffiliated hardware dealers to join cooperatives in the last decade. The revenue of the top five wholesale hardware cooperatives has grown 34 percent since 1992. The two largest, Ace Hardware Corp. and TruServ, supply 15,000 retail stores, which generate $27 billion in annual sales, just under one-fifth of the total market for hardware and building supplies.[4]

Hardware stores have experienced casualties as a result of the expansion of Home Depot, Lowe's, and other large chains, but cooperative membership has helped others stay afloat and sharpen their competitive edge. Ace Hardware's experience in Atlanta has been fairly typical. As Home Depot grew, Ace lost 30 of its 90 stores, but the cooperative helped the remainder modernize their stores and improve customer service. The result is that even with fewer stores Ace's market share in Atlanta is actually higher now than before Home Depot's expansion.[5]

The Independent Grocers Alliance (IGA) has had a similar experience. IGA's membership declined from 2,700 to 2,000 over the last ten years as independent grocers went out of business, but those that survived became more competitive. The average IGA store now generates $5.2 million in annual sales, up from $3.3 million a decade ago.[6]

Wholesale cooperatives cannot completely match the efficiency of chain stores, which have centralized control and decisionmaking, and stock a virtually identical mix of merchandise in each of their stores. Cooperative members, by contrast, vary widely in their operations and individually tailor their own inventory. Hardware stores, for instance, carry an average of 15,000 items. Each store in a cooperative will differ in the type and mix of products it offers, which reduces efficiency and raises costs for the cooperative.[7]

Grocery stores, like hardware stores, have a long history with cooperatives. Today about 15,000 grocers belong to a wholesale cooperative. Over the last decade, coops have emerged and expanded in other sectors as well, including pharmacy, office supplies, video, carpet, appliance, and camping equipment stores.

Wholesale cooperatives aren't the only option for small businesses. Some trade associations that represent independent retailers are finding ways for their members to cooperate on marketing, purchasing, and other joint ventures. These efforts can capture economies of scale and competitive advantages otherwise unavailable to small businesses.

The American Booksellers Association, for instance, is helping its members launch a web venture (Booksense.com) that will enable independent bookstores to compete for online book sales, a fast-growing market that has largely bypassed independents. The "back end" functions—the database, search engine, and transaction mechanism—will be shared and linked to each bookstore's own web site, allowing it to offer interactive browsing and sales functions as sophisticated as Amazon.com while retaining its distinct identity.

Other independent businesses are cooperating through cross-sector community-based business alliances. The Boulder Independent Business Alliance pioneered this approach in 1998 and now represents more than 125 locally owned businesses in Boulder, Colorado. In addition to representing independent businesses in public policy discussions and in the media, the alliance promotes its members through joint advertising and marketing efforts that encourage consumers to strengthen their community by patronizing local stores. Participating businesses also benefit from member to member discounts, such as reduced rates on advertising through local independent media outlets. Future endeavors may include a pooled insurance program and the formation of community investment fund.

Conclusion

As we have seen, the decline of locally owned retail businesses is not inevitable, nor is it solely the result of economic forces. Public policies all too often favor national retailers over homegrown businesses. Local merchants are disadvantaged by lax antitrust policies that allow large companies to unfairly exercise market power, by local zoning and economic development policies that encourage or subsidize the construction of chain stores, and by state and federal laws that fail to protect the interests and independence of small franchise businesses.

It is time to change the rules. A number of independent business associations and communities are leading the way, developing strategies and model policies that defend and nurture the homegrown economy.

Independent retail trade associations and cooperatives are growing more aggressive in their approach to competition from corporate retailers. Hardware dealers in the Upper Midwest, for instance, recently launched a series of advertisements encouraging consumers to patronize locally owned stores. The American Booksellers Association is providing an electronic infrastructure so its members can sell books over the Internet. Members of the Boulder Independent Business Alliance display bumper stickers that encourage consumers to "put your money where your house is" by shopping at local stores.

A number of independent business groups have gone a step further, taking their fight into the policy arena. The National Community Pharmacists Association, for instance, has helped enact laws in five states that bar HMOs from discriminating against independent pharmacies. The American Booksellers Association has challenged the predatory tactics of two bookstore chains in court, drawing attention to the need for a more vigorous approach to antitrust policy and enforcement. Franchisee associations have demanded state and federal rules to protect their autonomy. At the local level, independent merchants have fought land use and development policies that favor or subsidize their corporate competitors.

Citizens, planners, and policymakers are taking action as well. A number of communities have responded to the expansion of corporate chains by revising land use plans and zoning rules to favor locally owned, humanly scaled, diverse businesses. Often these efforts come on the heels of a fight; community coalitions that form to oppose a particular retail development have an opportunity to go a step further by pushing for new rules that eliminate the need for such fights in the future.

Some communities, like Kent County, Maryland, and Manchester, Vermont, have adopted comprehensive plans that overtly state a preference for locally owned businesses. Towns in New York, Connecticut, Ohio, Georgia,

Florida, Massachusetts and California have enacted zoning laws that limit the size of retail businesses. Palm Beach, Florida has developed an ordinance that ensures that businesses serve the communities where they are located.

Determined to retain their distinct character and sense of place, several communities in California, along with Bainbridge Island, Washington, and Sanibel Island, Florida, have enacted local ordinances that outlaw formula restaurants. Solvang, California, one of the towns to ban chain restaurants, also proposed a ban on formula retail establishments. Though not enacted, the proposal provides a useful model for other communities concerned about the proliferation of national chains.

Elsewhere, citizens have concluded that large scale retail developments warrant regional oversight. In Cape Cod, a regional planning agency is charged with reviewing proposals for new businesses that exceed a certain size. The agency's guidelines call for rejecting developments that harm the local economy, environment, or community character, while favoring those that are locally owned and employ Cape Cod residents. Vermont adopted regional planning on a statewide level with Act 250, which requires large commercial developments to demonstrate they will not adversely affect the environment or economy, or place unreasonable fiscal burdens on local governments.

There are doubtless many other rules communities could craft that would encourage a homegrown economy. Chain store taxes, for instance, were once enacted by more than half the states. Today cities or states could adopt graduated business license fees that increase according to the size of a retail chain.

By designing policies that put community first, local businesses can once again become a key component in a healthy, dynamic, and rooted retail sector.

Notes

CHAPTER one

1 "Five Hundred Largest U.S. Corporations," *Fortune*, April 26, 1999, p. F-1; "Top 100 Retailers," *Stores*, National Retail Federation, July 1999; Dana Canedy, "Supersizing the Supermarkets in a Shift of Power," *The New York Times*, November 13, 1998, p. C1.

2 A few of these stores, especially older outlets, are smaller (50,000 to 90,000 square feet). The average Wal-Mart is about 100,000 square feet, but the trend has been towards ever larger stores. Almost all of the Wal-Mart stores built in the last couple of years have exceeded 100,000 square feet and the retailer is regularly constructing stores with more than 200,000 square feet of space.

3 John Seeley, "Independents Throw Book at Behemoths: Local Booksellers Join Suit Against National Chains," *LA Weekly*, May 1, 1998, p. 12; Anika M. Scott, "Small Bookstores Write New Chapter in War with Giants: Many Independent Booksellers Stay Alive by Catering to a Specialty Audience," *Chicago Tribune*, August 24, 1998, p. 3.

4 Ron Devlin, "Prices, Selection Identify the Category Super-Store: The phenomenon has emerged solidly in sneakers, hardware, office supplies, computers and stereos, grocery shopping and even the movies," *The (Allentown, PA) Morning Call*, February 23, 1997, p. A7; Jennifer Steinhauer, "Getting the Chance To Do It Himself: Out of the Shadows to Run Home Depot," *The New York Times*, May 13, 1998, p. D1.

5 Carol Emert, "Staying Alive Amid Office Superstores," *The San Francisco Chronicle*, June 20, 1998, p. E1.

6 Genevieve Buck, "Deal No Cure for Druggists' Ache," *Chicago Tribune*, July 17, 1998, Business Section, p. 1; Susan Riley and Julie Hough, "Business watch: pharmaceutical industry," *Medical Marketing & Media*, May 1998, p. 50.

7 "Starbucks Has Disappointing December," *The New York Times*, January 5, 1999, p. C2; Seth Goldstein, "Indie Video Retailers Plan Suit Against Studios, Blockbuster," *Billboard*, July 18, 1998.

8 "Top 100," *Nation's Restaurant News*, June 23, 1997, p. 102.

9 Chris Woodyard, "Small firms 'roll up' into the big leagues," *USA Today*, March 23, 1998, p. B1.

10 J. F. Hornbeck, "The Discount Retail Industry and Its Effect on Small Towns and Rural Communities," *Congressional Research Service Report for Congress*, January 18, 1994, p. 6.

11 William H. Borghesani, Peter L. de la Cruz, and David B. Berry, "Controlling the chain:

buyer power, distributive control, and new dynamics in retailing," *Business Horizons*, Indiana University, July 17, 1997, p. 17.

[12] "Wholesale Food Distribution: Today and Tomorrow," Report of the National-American Wholesale Grocers Association, 1993, p. 37; Canedy, *The New York Times*, November 13, 1998, p. C1.

[13] Quoted in Constance E. Beaumont, *Better Models for Superstores: Alternatives to Big-Box Sprawl*, National Trust for Historic Preservation, 1997, p. 4.

[14] Doreen Carvajal, "Once Upon a Frenzy: Book Industry in Big Shift Focused on Product Delivery," *The New York Times*, November 18, 1998, p. C1.

[15] Matthew Schifrin, "The Big Squeeze," *Forbes*, March 11, 1996, p. 45.

[16] Schifrin, *Forbes*, March 11, 1996, p. 45; Zachary Schiller, Wendy Zellner, and Ron Stodghill, "Clout! More and More, Retail Giants Rule the Marketplace," *Business Week*, December 21, 1992, p. 66.

[17] Quoted in Schifrin, *Forbes*, March 11, 1996.

[18] Lionel Diaz, Senior Vice President, Manufacturers' Agents National Association, Testimony before the Committee on Small Business, U.S. House of Representatives, August 10, 1994.

[19] David Morris, "Bits, Bytes & Community," *Groundwork*, Spring 1998, p. 14-15; Susan Feyder, "Indications of a continuing Internet infatuation," *Minneapolis Star Tribune*, May 24, 1999, p.1D.

CHAPTER two

[1] "The Impact of Superstores on Small Business: A Case Study of Wal-Mart," Testimony by Thomas Muller at the hearings of the Committee on Small Business, U.S. House of Representatives, August 10, 1994.

[2] Elizabeth Humstone and Thomas Muller, "Impact of Wal-Mart Stores on Northwestern Vermont," prepared for the Preservation Trust of Vermont, the Vermont Natural Resources Council, and Williston Citizens for Responsible Growth, September 1995, p. 14.

[3] Chris Roush, "Home Depot using predato-

ry pricing tactics, critics say," *Atlanta Journal & Constitution*, March 18, 1995, p. 1B.

[4] William H. Borghesani, Peter L. de la Cruz, and David B. Berry, "Controlling the chain: buyer power, distributive control, and new dynamics in retailing," *Business Horizons*, Indiana University, July 17, 1997, p. 17.

[5] David L. Kurtz, Scott B. Keller, Mike J. Landry and Daniel F. Lynch, "Wal-Mart fights the battle of Conway: Arkansas predatory pricing suit," *Business Horizons*, September 1995, p. 46; Norman W. Hawker, "Wal-Mart and the Divergence of State and Federal Predatory Pricing Law," *Journal of Public Policy & Marketing*, Spring 1996, p. 141.

[6] Thomas Muller and Elizabeth Humstone, "What Happened When Wal-Mart Came to Town? A Report on Three Iowa Communities with a Statistical Analysis of Seven Iowa Counties," The National Trust for Historic Preservation, May 1996, p. 8; Similar results were reached in "Competing With the Discount Mass Merchandisers," a study by Dr. Kenneth E. Stone, Iowa State University, 1995.

[7] Studies by Dr. Kenneth Stone of Iowa State University have found that the brunt of Wal-Mart's impact in Iowa has been felt in towns of less than 5,000 located within 20 miles of the retailer. "Competing With the Discount Mass Merchandisers," p. 21.

[8] Bob Doucette, "Warr Acres Expects Decline In Funds," *The Daily Oklahoman*, November 23, 1998, Community Section, p. 1; "Warr Acres Mayor Defends Escrow Plan," *The Daily Oklahoman*, January 20, 1992, Community Section, p. 2.

[9] "The Portable Wal-Mart," *Sprawl-Busters Alert*, April 1999; Mark P. Couch, "Big-box stores often empty, study says: Giant retail stores responsible for 60 percent of KC's unused floor space," *The Kansas City Star*, March 16, 1999, p. D6.

[10] Bernadette Tansey, "Costco Plots Move From Martinez to Concord," *The San Francisco Chronicle*, August 25, 1998, p. A11.

[11] Dr. Edward B. Shils, Director Emeritus, Wharton Entrepreneurial Center, University of Pennsylvania, "Measuring the Economic and Sociological Impact of the Mega-Retail Discount Chains on Small Enterprise in Urban, Suburban and Rural Communities," published on the web at www.shilsreport.org, February 7, 1997.

[12] "Johnstown, NY: Wal-Mart Welfare," *Sprawl-Busters Alert*, November 1998.

[13] Douglas P. Shuit, "The Retail Wags the Dog: As cities vie for the big sales tax producers that can help keep budgets afloat, legislation is being considered to save them from themselves," *Los Angeles Times*, July 17, 1998, p. B2.

[14] Land Use, Inc. and RKG Associates, "Greenfield, Massachusetts: Fiscal & Economic Impact Assessment of the Proposed Wal-Mart Development," April 2, 1993.

[15] Town of North Elba Planning Board, "Statement of Findings and Decision: Proposed Wal-Mart Store," January 9, 1996, p. 14.

[16] Elizabeth Humstone and Thomas Muller, "Impact of Wal-Mart Stores on Northwestern Vermont," p. 40, 45, and 47.

[17] Vermont Environmental Board, Re: St. Albans Group and Wal*Mart Stores, Inc., Findings of Fact, Conclusions of Law, and Order (Altered), Application #6F0471-EB, June 27, 1995, p. 1.

[18] "Competing With the Discount Mass Merchandisers," a study by Dr. Kenneth E. Stone, Iowa State University, 1995, p. 19.

[19] Town of North Elba Planning Board, "Statement of Findings and Decision: Proposed Wal-Mart Store," January 9, 1996, p. 15.

[20] Patricia A. Frishkoff and Alicja M. Kostecka, "Business Contributions to Community Service," Office of Advocacy, U.S. Small Business Administration, October 1991.

CHAPTER three

[1] For a detailed discussion of the evolution of antitrust policy, see Michael J. Sandel, *Democracy's Discontent: America in Search of a Public Philosophy*, Cambridge: Harvard University Press, 1996, p. 231-249.

[2] Quoted in Sandel, *Democracy's Discontent*, p. 232.

[3] Quoted in Sandel, *Democracy's Discontent*, p. 243.

[4] Walter Adams and James W. Brock, "Areeda / Turner on Antitrust: a Hobson's choice," *Antitrust Bulletin*, December 1996, p. 735, quoting Phillip Areeda and Donald Turner, *Antitrust Law: An Analysis of Antitrust Principles and Their Application*, Boston: Little, Brown, 1978, Vol. I, p. 7.

[5] Northeastern Tel. Co. v. American Tel. & Tel. Co., 455 U.S. 943 (1982), quoted in Jonathan Moore Peterson, "Taming the Sprawlmart: Using an Antitrust Arsenal to Further Historic Preservation Goals," *Urban Lawyer*, Spring 1995, footnote 45.

[6] For a discussion of the case see Peterson, *Urban Lawyer*, Spring 1995, or Norman W. Hawker, "Wal-Mart and the Divergence of State and Federal Predatory Pricing Law," *Journal of Public Policy & Marketing*, Spring 1996, p. 141.

[7] Gregory T. Gundlach, "Price Predation: Legal Limits and Antitrust Considerations," *Journal of Public Policy and Marketing*, Fall 1995, p. 278.

[8] Kenneth Glazer, "Predatory Pricing and Beyond: Life After Brooke Group," *Antitrust Law Journal*, March 22, 1994, p. 605.

[9] Terry Calvani and Gilde Breidenbach, "Living with the Robinson-Patman Act: Selected Articles: An Introduction to the Robinson-Patman Act and Its Enforcement by the Government," *Antitrust Law Journal*, 1990-91.

[10] Donald S. Clark, Secretary, Federal Trade Commission, "The Robinson-Patman Act: Annual Update," before the Robinson-Patman Act Committee Section of Antitrust Law, Forty-Sixth Annual Spring Meeting, Washington, DC, April 2, 1998.

[11] Richard J. Wegener, "Ninth Circuit decision invites high court to resolve circuit split on rebuttability of competitive injury inference under Robinson-Patman price discrimination act," *The National Law Journal*, May 19, 1997, p. B5.

[12] Quoted in David Balto, "In Defense of Robinson-Patman: In Defense of Small Business," *Legal Times*, October 13, 1997, p. 23.

[13] Chroma Lighting v. GTE Products Corp., 9th Cir., 1997.

[14] William H. Borghesani, Peter L. de la Cruz, and David B. Berry, "Controlling the chain: buyer power, distributive control, and new dynamics in retailing," *Business Horizons*, Indiana University, July 17, 1997, p. 17;

William E. Kovacic, "Downsizing Antitrust: Is It Time to End Dual Federal Enforcement?" *Antitrust Bulletin,* September 1996, p. 505.

[15] Complaint filed by the American Booksellers Association, Inc. against Barnes & Noble, Inc. and Borders Group, Inc. in U.S. District Court for the Northern District of California, April 1998.

[16] Josh Geltin, "Battle with Big Bookstores Puts Independents in Bind," *Los Angeles Times,* April 28, 1998, p. A-1; John F. Baker, "ABA Sues Barnes & Noble and Borders," *Publishers Weekly,* March 18, 1998.

[17] Quoted in complaint filed by the American Booksellers Association, April 1998.

[18] Donald S. Clark, Secretary, Federal Trade Commission, "The Robinson-Patman Act: Annual Update," before the Robinson-Patman Act Committee Section of Antitrust Law, 46th Annual Spring Meeting, Washington DC, April 2, 1998; Donald S. Clark, Secretary, Federal Trade Commission, "The Robinson-Patman Act: General Principles, Commission Proceedings, and Selected Issues," speech before the Ambit Group Retail Channel Conference for the Computer Industry, San Jose, CA, June 7, 1995.

[19] FTC Order, Sept. 10, 1996.

[20] Nick Gillespie, "Borders Patrol: Competition in the Book Industry," *Reason,* July 1995, p. 37.

[21] Interview with David Unowsky, "Mid Morning," Minnesota Public Radio, October 20, 1998; John Seeley, "Independents Throw Book at Behemoths: Local Booksellers Join Suit Against National Chains," *LA Weekly,* May 1, 1998, p. 12.

[22] John Mutter, "One size doesn't fit all: Ever more stores stuffed with ever more books causes ever more anxiety," *Publishers Weekly,* January 6, 1997, p. 40; Megan Schnabel, "Superstores have opened a new chapter in bookselling: Consumers win, small operators lose," *Roanoke Times & World News,* March 22, 1998, Business Section, p. 1. Internet booksellers are collecting promotional fees as well. Amazon.com charges up to $12,500 for the placement of a title. John Mutter and Steven M. Zeitchik, "Co-op policies of online retailers under scrutiny," *Publishers Weekly,* February 15, 1999, p. 10.

[23] "Superstores, Megabooks and Humongous Headaches," *Business Week,* April 14, 1997, p. 92.

[24] Complaint filed by the American Booksellers Association, April 1998.

[25] Complaint filed by the American Booksellers Association, April 1998.

[26] Quoted in John Rosengren, "The Battle of the Bookstores," *Minneapolis-St. Paul City Business,* July 31, 1998, p. 26.

[27] Daniel Kadlec, "How Blockbuster Changed The Rules: How's this for a strategy? Give the customers the hot products they want. Sounds simple, and it's at the core of the company's sharp turnaround," *Time,* August 3, 1998, p. 48.

[28] Seth Goldstein, "Indie Video Retailers Plan Suit Against Studios, Blockbuster," *Billboard,* July 18, 1998; Paul Sweeting, "Major Squeeze Play Put on Indie Videos," *Variety,* August 3 - 9, 1998, p. 12.

[29] Dave McNary, "Erasing Mom and Pop: Independent video stores feeling squeezed by big-chain rental barns," *The Daily News of Los Angeles,* March 28, 1999, p. B1.

[30] The exact nature of the state laws vary, and some, depending on the criteria, may or may not be counted in a given list. The 24 referred to here are Arkansas, California, Colorado, Hawaii, Idaho, Kentucky, Louisiana, Maine, Maryland, Massachusetts, Minnesota, Montana, Nebraska, North Carolina, North Dakota, Oklahoma, Pennsylvania, Rhode Island, South Carolina, Tennessee, Utah, West Virginia, Wisconsin, and Wyoming.

[31] Hawker, *Journal of Public Policy & Marketing,* Spring 1996.

[32] Quoted in Peterson, *Urban Lawyer,* Spring 1995.

[33] A few states require evidence of harm to competition, rather than simply intent to injure competition. Hawker, *Journal of Public Policy & Marketing,* Spring 1996; Peterson, *Urban Lawyer,* Spring 1995.

[34] Chris Roush, "Home Depot using predatory pricing tactics, critics say," *Atlanta Journal & Constitution,* March 18, 1995, p. 1B.

[35] Dr. Edward B. Shils, Director Emeritus, Wharton Entrepreneurial Center, University of Pennsylvania, "Measuring the Eco-

nomic and Sociological Impact of the Mega-Retail Discount Chains on Small Enterprise in Urban, Suburban and Rural Communities," published on the web at www.shilsreport.org, February 7, 1997.

[36] Hawker, *Journal of Public Policy & Marketing*, Spring 1996; David L. Kurtz, Scott B. Keller, Mike J. Landry, and Daniel F. Lynch, "Wal-Mart fights the battle of Conway, Arkansas predatory pricing suit," *Business Horizons*, September 1995, p. 46.

[37] Text of the Wal-Mart Ruling by the Supreme Court of Arkansas, reprinted in the *Arkansas Democrat-Gazette*, January 10, 1995, p. 3B.

CHAPTER four

[1] Quoted in Kris Sherman, "Wal-Mart Gives Up Plans for Gig Harbor: Foes Declare Victory Over Retailing Giant," *The (Tacoma, WA) News Tribune*, November 22, 1996, p. A1.

[2] Details on the examples provided here and many others are available in Sprawl-Buster's monthly newsletter or on the group's web site at www.sprawl-busters.com.

[3] Sprawl-Busters, "Money Vs. Community," *NewsFlash!*, April 10, 1999; Sprawl-Busters, "Another Wal-Mart Referendum," *NewsFlash!*, February 1, 1999.

[4] Thomas Scheffey, "Fighting 'Sprawl-Mart,'" *The Connecticut Law Tribune*, December 25, 1995 - January 1, 1996, p. 1; Thomas J. Quinn, "Kmart Continues Court Fight to Build Westlake Store," *The (Cleveland) Plain Dealer*, August 27, 1997, p. 2B.

[5] San Francisco Planning Code, Sec. 722.1.

[6] Quoted in Constance E. Beaumont, *How Superstore Sprawl Can Harm Communities, and What Citizens Can Do About It*, National Trust for Historic Preservation, 1994, p. 22.

[7] Quoted in Constance E. Beaumont, *Better Models for Superstores: Alternatives to Big-Box Sprawl*, National Trust for Historic Preservation, 1997, p. 36.

[8] Town Plan, Town of Manchester, Vermont, adopted November 18, 1997, p. 15-18.

[9] Arthur W. Hooper and Howard Goldman,

"Where the 'Big Boxes' Belong," *The National Law Journal*, March 18, 1996, p. B7.

[10] Some states, such as New Jersey, forbid development moratoria. Beaumont, *Better Models for Superstores*, 1997, p. 40-41.

[11] Jonathan Walters, "Store Wars," *Governing Magazine*, January 1995, p. 28.

[12] Jane Kwiatkowski, "Williamsville follows trend by issuing building ban," *The Buffalo News*, August 16, 1997, p. 5C.

[13] The text of many of the ordinances presented here can be found in the Main Streets section of the New Rules web site at www.newrules.org.

[14] Beaumont, *Better Models for Superstores*, 1997, p. 3.

[15] Noel Dempsey, Minister for the Environment and Local Government, General Policy Directive (Shopping), S.I. No.193 of 1998; Roddy O'Sullivan, "Superstores in limbo until Dempsey conducts study," *The Irish Times*, September 25, 1998.

[16] Town of Skaneateles Local Law No. 1 of 1994.

[17] Quoted in Kwiatkowski, *The Buffalo News*, August 16, 1997.

[18] Town of Westford, Amendment to Zoning Bylaw, Section 173-11, October 24, 1994.

[19] Local law to amend the Town of North Elba Land Use Code (Local Law No. 1 of the year 1977, as amended) in various respects, February 1998.

[20] Daniela Altimari, "Huge stores, sizable clamor: Community activists try to zone out the 'big box,'" *The Hartford Courant*, October 5, 1996, p. F1.

[21] Beaumont, *Better Models for Superstores*, 1997, p. 38.

[22] Jay Croft, "Developer suing Roswell: Lengthy dispute: Proponents of a Target superstore accuse city officials of zoning shenanigans," *The Atlanta Journal and Constitution*, April 16, 1998, p. 3JH.

[23] Jon Steinman and Rich McKay, "Superstore Battle Zones: DeLand is not alone in controversy over Wal-Mart," *The Orlando Sentinel*, April 25, 1999, p. K1.

[24] Plymouth Zoning Bylaw, Section 401.12, General Commercial; Jeff McLaughlin, "Home Depot is denied permit in Plymouth," *The Boston Globe*, April 26, 1998,

p. 7; John O'Keefe, "Denial of permit for Home Depot is appealed," *The Patriot Ledger*, June 2, 1998, p. 6S; Alexander Reid, "Village fears impact of huge store: Scale questioned, while Plymouth needs the taxes," *The Boston Globe*, February 1, 1998, South Weekly Section, p. 1.

25 Beaumont, *Better Models for Superstores*, 1997, p. 39.

26 Tanya Schevitz, "Novato to consider 'big' business permit," *(Novato, CA) Independent Journal*, January 13, 1997, p. B1.

27 Alan D. Miller, "Chardon Stands Up to Wal-Mart—and Wins," *The Columbus Dispatch*, March 14, 1998, p. 1A.

28 Peter Roland, Residents for Responsible Growth (Lake Placid, NY), conversation with author, January 14, 1999.

29 Marya Morris, "Taking the bite out of big projects: state and regional agencies are fine-tuning regulations governing developments of regional impact," *Planning*, February 1997, p. 20.

30 Patrick Butler, "The Cape Cod Commission—Five Years Later," *Massachusetts Lawyers Weekly*, September 30, 1996, p. B5.

31 "1996 Final Regional Policy Plan," approved by the Barnstable County Assembly of Delegates and County Commissioners, November 1996, available on the web at www.capecodcommission.org.

32 "1996 Final Regional Policy Plan."

33 Sylvia Lewis, "When Wal-Mart Says 'Uncle,'" *Planning*, August 1994, p. 15; Elizabeth Ross, "Cape Cod Resists Next Wave: Superstores," *The Christian Science Monitor*, August 1, 1994, p. 8; Beaumont, *Better Models for Superstores*, 1997, p. 42.

34 Beaumont, *Better Models for Superstores*, 1997, p. 42.

35 "1996 Final Regional Policy Plan."

36 Act 250 is available on the Vermont Environmental Board's web site at www.state.vt.us/envboard.

37 Vermont's Land Use and Development Law, 10 V.S.A. § 6086, "Issuance of permit; conditions and criteria."

38 Beaumont, *Better Models for Superstores*, 1997, p. 17-21; "Wal-Mart store holds grand opening in Berlin," The Associated Press, January 28, 1999.

39 Vermont Supreme Court, In re Wal-Mart Stores, Inc. and The St. Albans Group (95-398), August 29, 1997.

40 Town Plan, Town of Manchester, Vermont, adopted November 18, 1997, p. 5-10.

41 Schedule of Use Regulations, Palm Beach.

42 Handelsman v. Town of Palm Beach, District Court of Appeal of Florida, Fourth District, October 16, 1991.

43 Rick Tooker, Carmel Community Building and Planning Department, conversation with author, June 17, 1998; Carmel Laws, Chapter 17.06, Definitions, p. 06-29.

44 Quoted in David Ammons, "Washington Island Opposes Starbucks," The Associated Press, May 3, 1998; City of Winslow (former name of Bainbridge), Ordinance No. 89-28.

45 Solvang Ordinance No. 94-151, adopted May 9, 1994.

46 Pacific Grove Ordinance 1999 N.S. § 3, 1995.

47 Quoted in Gerrie Ferris, "Sanibel banning formula food," *The Atlanta Journal and Constitution*, September 19, 1996, p. 02D.

48 Quoted in Irene Lelchuk, "Solvang divided over growth: Merchants fear city's proposed plan for outlet center," *Santa Maria Times*, January 15, 1995, p. B-7.

49 "Report from the Formula Retail / Growth Management Task Force," Solvang, California, July 1995; "Solvang Formula Retail / Growth Management Task Force - Minority Opinion," June 30, 1995, p. 1.

50 "Solvang Formula Retail / Growth Management Task Force - Minority Opinion," p. 5.

51 "Solvang Formula Retail / Growth Management Task Force - Minority Opinion," p. 6.

52 "Report from the Formula Retail / Growth Management Task Force," p. 12.

53 "Solvang Formula Retail / Growth Management Task Force - Minority Opinion," p. 11.

54 "Solvang Formula Retail / Growth Management Task Force - Minority Opinion," p. 13.

CHAPTER five

1 Ryan Mathews, "The depression and beyond; history of Super Valu Stores Inc. through the depression years," *Grocery Marketing*, August 1992, p. SV24; Terry Calvani and Gilde Breidenbach, "An Introduction to the Robinson-Patman Act and Its Enforcement by the Government," *Antitrust Law Journal*, Developments 1990-91, Vol. 59, No. 761; Charles F. Phillips, "The Chain Store in the United States and Canada," *The American Economic Review*, 1937, p. 87-95.

2 Thomas W. Ross, "Winners and Losers Under the Robinson-Patman Act," *Journal of Law and Economics*, October 1984, p. 246.

3 Michael J. Sandel, *Democracy's Discontent: America in Search of a Public Philosophy*, Cambridge: Harvard University Press, 1996, p. 227-231.

4 Quoted in Sandel, *Democracy's Discontent*, p. 229.

5 Calvani and Breidenbach, *Antitrust Law Journal*, 1990-91.

6 Ross, *Journal of Law and Economics*, October 1984, p. 247; A few states, notably Maryland, enacted laws banning new chain stores units within their borders, but these were struck down by the courts. See Joseph Cornwall Palamountain, Jr., *The Politics of Distribution*, Cambridge: Harvard University Press, 1955, p. 161.

7 Robert E. Cushman, "Constitutional Law in 1930-31," *The American Political Science Review*, 1931, p. 78-80.

8 Palamountain, *The Politics of Distribution*, see footnote 17, p. 165.

9 Thomas W. Ross, "Store Wars: The Chain Tax Movement," *Journal of Law and Economics*, April 1986, p. 126.

10 Ross, *Journal of Law and Economics*, April 1986, p. 126.

11 Palamountain, *The Politics of Distribution*, p. 166.

12 D.F. Dixon, "Gasoline Marketing in the United States: The First Fifty Years," *Journal of Industrial Economics*, November 1964, p. 23-42.

13 Willard L. Thorp, "Changing Distribution Channels," *The American Economic Review*, 1939, p. 81; Palamountain, *The Politics of Distribution*, p. 167.

14 Ross, *Journal of Law and Economics*, October 1984, p. 247.

15 Ross, *Journal of Law and Economics*, April 1986, p. 127.

16 Palamountain, *The Politics of Distribution*, p. 167.

17 Ross *Journal of Law and Economics*, October 1984, p. 258.

18 Donald F. Dixon, "Inter-war changes in gasoline distribution: A U.S.-UK comparison," *Business & Economic History*, Winter 1997, p. 632-648.

19 Ross, *Journal of Law and Economics*, October 1984, p. 248-249.

20 Calvani and Breidenbach, *Antitrust Law Journal*, 1990-91; Ross, *Journal of Law and Economics*, October 1984, p. 248-249.

21 Sandel, *Democracy's Discontent*, p. 230-231.

22 Ross, *Journal of Law and Economics*, April 1986, p. 127.

23 Bob Ortega, *In Sam We Trust: The Untold Story of Sam Walton and How Wal-Mart is Devouring America*, New York: Random House, 1998, p. 42.

24 It seems unlikely that the Supreme Court would have upheld this portion of the legislation as the Court overturned a similar provision in Florida's chain store tax law that was based on whether a chain extended into more than one county (Louis K. Liggett Co. v. Lee (1933)).

25 Palamountain, *The Politics of Distribution*, p. 176.

26 Ross, *Journal of Law and Economics*, October 1984, p. 249.

27 Today, chain store taxes can be found in a few places, but most are extremely mild. The city of Shreveport in Louisiana, for instance, levies an annual business license tax on chain stores, which ranges from $10 for stores in systems with two units to $550 for those with more than 500 outlets. The city calculates the tax rate based on the total number of units owned and managed by the company worldwide. Charter of the City of Shreveport, "Chain Store Tax," Chapter 86, Article IV.

28 Palamountain, *The Politics of Distribution*, p. 186.

CHAPTER SIX

1 Robin Lee Allen, "The NRN 50: The Franchisees," *Nation's Restaurant News*, January 1, 1998, p. 12.

2 Robin Lee Allen, *Nation's Restaurant News*, January 1, 1998, p. 12; Richard C. Hoffman and John F. Preble, "Franchising in the twenty-first century," *Business Horizons*, November 1993, p. 35.

3 Karen M. Lundegaard, "Investing in a franchise doesn't guarantee immediate success," *The (San Jose) Business Journal*, November 17, 1997.

4 Christina Fulop and Jim Forward, "Insights into franchising: A review of empirical and theoretical perspectives," *Service Industries Journal*, October 1997, p. 603-625.

5 "Buying a franchise," *USA Today*, August 31, 1998, p. 1B.

6 David Hess, "The Iowa Franchise Act: Towards Protecting Reasonable Expectations of Franchisees and Franchisors," *Iowa Law Review*, 1995, p. 338 (see footnote 40).

7 Robert Purvin, Jr., *The Franchise Fraud: How to Protect Yourself Before and After You Invest*, John Wiley & Sons, 1994.

8 Dean M. Sagar, Congressional Aide to Representative John J. LaFalce (D-NY), conversation with author, April 8, 1998.

9 Robert L. Purvin, Jr., franchise attorney and president of the American Association of Franchisees and Dealers, Prepared Statement presented at the Hearing on Franchising in the U.S. Economy before the Small Business Committee, U.S. House of Representatives, September 27, 1990.

10 "Franchise Industry Research and Data," Staff Memorandum submitted to Congressman John J. LaFalce, Chairman of the Small Business Committee, U.S. House of Representatives, 1992, p. 1-6.

11 "Franchise Industry Research and Data," p. 8-10.

12 Dr. Timothy Bates, "Survival Patterns Among Franchise and Nonfranchise Firms Started in 1986 and 1987," U.S. Small Business Administration, 1996.

13 Quoted in "Franchise Industry Research and Data," p. 10.

14 Dean M. Sagar, Congressional Aide to Representative John J. LaFalce (D-NY), conversation with author, April 8, 1998.

15 Andrew C. Selden, franchise attorney, Statement before the Small Business Committee, U.S. House of Representatives, July 21, 1992, p. 8.

16 Samuel Crawford, American Franchisee Association, conversation with author, April 3, 1998.

17 Selden, Statement, July 21, 1992, p. 7.

18 Selden, Statement, July 21, 1992, p. 8.

19 Selden, Statement, July 21, 1992, p. 5.

20 "Franchise Industry Research and Data," p. 22-23.

21 Robin Lee Allen, *Nation's Restaurant News*, January 1, 1998, p. 12.

22 Federal Trade Commission, "Disclosure Requirements and Prohibitions Concerning Franchising and Business Opportunity Ventures," 16 CFR Part 436.

23 "Franchise Industry Research and Data," p. 26-27.

24 Carrie Mason-Draffen, "Heaven and Hell: For some franchising is a dream come true; for others it's their worst nightmare," *New York Newsday*, August 28, 1994, p. A88.

25 Statement of Susan P. Kezios, President of the American Franchisee Association, before the Subcommittee on Transportation and Hazardous Materials, Committee on Energy and Commerce, U.S. House of Representatives, August 3, 1994.

26 "Franchise Industry Research and Data," p. 26.

27 Joan Oleck, "The Battle of Iowa: How the Biggest Franchise Fight in History was Won - and Lost," *Restaurant Business*, August 10, 1992, p. 90.

28 Quoted in Robin Lee Allen, "The Franchisees: American Food Industries," *The Nation's Restaurant News*, January 1, 1998, p. 16.

29 "Chart of Laws Reported," *Business Franchise Guide*, Chicago: Commerce Clearing House, 1998, paragraph 2001.

30 See Indiana's "Deceptive Franchise Practices" statute, Indiana Code, Title 23, Article 2, Chapter 2.7, Sec. 1 (1).

31 Ron Gardner, franchise attorney, conversation with author, September 28, 1998; Arkansas Statute Section 70-807.

32 "Franchise Industry Research and Data," p. 52; 70.

33 California's 1980 franchise act was the last franchise relationship law prior to Iowa's.

34 Hess, *Iowa Law Review*, 1995, p. 359.

35 Iowa Code 523H.6. Enacted 1992, amended 1995.

36 Iowa Code 523H.5. Enacted 1992, amended 1995.

37 Iowa Code 523H.11. Enacted 1992, amended 1995.

38 Iowa Code 523H.12. Enacted 1992, amended 1995.

39 Iowa Code 523H.7. Enacted 1992, amended 1995.

40 Steven p. Rosenfeld, "Franchisors claim partial victory in battle over restrictive Iowa law," The Associated Press, July 12, 1994.

41 Jackie King, "Iowa Franchise Act in National Light," *Business Record*, August 1, 1994.

42 King, *Business Record*, August 1, 1994; Elbert David, "Support grows for franchise reforms," *The Des Moines Register*, February 22, 1994, p. B6.

43 Hess, *Iowa Law Review*, 1995, p. 351.

44 Andrew Selden, franchise attorney, conversation with author, September 28, 1998.

45 Hess, *Iowa Law Review*, 1995, p. 353 (see footnote 157).

46 Hess, *Iowa Law Review*, 1995, p. 347-350.

47 Automobile Dealers Franchise Act of 1956, 15 U.S.C. 1221-1225; Federal Petroleum Marketing Practices Act of 1978, 15 U.S.C. 2801-2806.

48 "Franchise Industry Research and Data," p. 76.

49 Scott A. Hodge, "For Big Franchisers, Money to Go: Is the SBA Dispensing Corporate Welfare?" *The Washington Post*, November 30, 1997, p. C01;

50 Quoted in Robin Lee Allen, "Franchise Relations: Is It a More Level Playing Field," *Nation's Restaurant News*, October 14, 1996, p. 1.

51 Mike Stamler, U.S. Small Business Administration, conversation with author, April 6, 1998.

52 Robin Lee Allen, *Nation's Restaurant News*, October 14, 1996.

CHAPTER seven

1 James R. Hagerty, "Tough as Nails: Home Depot Raise the Ante, Targeting Mom-and-Pop Rivals," *The Wall Street Journal*, January 25, 1999, p. A1.

2 Barnaby J. Feder, "In Hardware War, Cooperation May Mean Survival: Independents Have a Weapon Against the 'Big Boxes,'" *The New York Times*, June 11, 1997, p. D1; Paul Hazen, National Cooperative Business Association, conversation with author, November 20, 1998.

3 Hagerty, *The Wall Street Journal*, January 25, 1999, p. A1.

4 National Cooperative Bank, *America's Top 100 Co-op Companies*, 1998, p. 7; Lorrie Grant, "Cooperatives vs. Superstores: Smaller rivals seek pricing power," *USA Today*, July 15, 1998, p. 4B; "TruServ Corp. Launches Real-time Inventory System With Internet Backbone, TransFuse Access Muscle," Business Wire, September 29, 1998.

5 Feder, *The New York Times*, June 11, 1997, p. D1.

6 Dana Canedy, "Supersizing the Supermarkets in a Shift of Power: Discounters and Mergers Alter Balance of Power," *The New York Times*, November 13, 1998, p. C1.

7 Mack Hardin, Minnesota-Dakotas Retail Hardware Association, conversation with author, November 16, 1998.

Appendix

Resources

Examples of the policies described in this publication—
including the full text of laws and relevant court cases,
background material, resources, links, and news—can be
found on the New Rules website at **www.newrules.org**.

For information and assistance organizing a community campaign to stop corporate retail development:

Sprawl-Busters
21 Grinnell Street
Greenfield, MA 01301
telephone: 413-772-6289
web: www.sprawl-busters.com

For strategies to revitalize Main Street:

The Main Street Center
National Trust for Historic Preservation
1785 Massachusetts Avenue NW
Washington, DC 20036
telephone: 202-588-6219
web: www.mainst.org

For information and assistance organizing a community-wide coalition of independent businesses:

Boulder Independent Business Alliance
PO Box 532
Boulder, CO 80306
telephone: 303-402-1575
web: www.boulder-iba.org

A number of trade associations represent and defend the interests of independent businesses, including:

American Booksellers Association
828 South Broadway
Tarrytown, NY 10591
telephone: 800-637-0037
web: www.bookweb.org/aba

National Community Pharmacists Association
205 Daingerfield Road
Alexandria, VA 22314
telephone: 800-544-7447
web: www.ncpanet.org

American Association of Franchisees and Dealers
PO Box 81887
San Diego, CA 92138
telephone: 800-733-9858
web: www.aafd.org

American Franchisee Association
53 West Jackson Boulevard, Suite 205
Chicago, IL 60604
telephone: 312- 431-0545

For information on retailer-owned purchasing and wholesale cooperatives:

National Cooperative Business Association
1401 New York Avenue NW, Suite 1100
Washington, DC 20005
telephone: 202-638-6222
web: www.cooperative.org

For information on regional planning:

Cape Cod Commission
PO Box 226
Barnstable, MA 02630
telephone: 508-362-3828
web: www.capecodcommission.org

Vermont Environmental Board
National Life Records Center Building
Drawer 20
Montpelier, VT 05620
telephone: 802-828-3309
web: www.state.vt.us/envboard/